CANTERBURY
A Pictorial History

The site of the Martyrdom in the cathedral where Archbishop Becket was murdered, photographed *c*.1907.

CANTERBURY
A Pictorial History

Ivan Green

Phillimore

1988

Published by
PHILLIMORE & CO. LTD.
Shopwyke Hall, Chichester, Sussex

ISBN 0 85033 668 6

Printed and bound in Great Britain by
BIDDLES LTD.
Guildford, Surrey

To Margaret

List of Illustrations

Acknowledgements

I should like to record my grateful thanks to many people, and organisations, who have helped in many ways, in particular to: English Heritage, the guardian of so many of our wonderful ancient buildings, and especially to two members of their staff, Stephen Carswell and Wilfred Smedley, both of whom have shared with me their own knowledge and love of the buildings to which they devote so much of their time; the Dean and Chapter for allowing me to photograph and publish the exterior views of the cathedral; the Canterbury library and its librarian, and especially to the reference librarian and local historian, David Cousins; Dr. Richard Stevens and Mary Stevens; Mrs. Frances Mee and the members of the team at Shopwyke Hall, and to the many people who over the years have given me, or lent to me for photographing, pictures and prints and who have also contributed information.

I hope they will understand that, unfortunately, certain material has had to be omitted due to the nature and scope of the subject.

I would like to thank the following for permission to reproduce illustrations in this book: English Heritage, nos. 2, 3, 18, 19, 20; Canterbury library, nos. 31, 34, 35, 41, 42, 46, 47, 50, 55, 59, 67, 86, 88, 90, 95, 96, 112, 113, 115, 116, 120, 122, 128, 132, 133, 134, 135, 136, 140, 146, 147, 150, 153, 155, 157, 158, 159, 164, 165; the Dean and Chapter of Canterbury, nos. 37, 38; Mr. George Bishop, no. 97. The remainder are my own photographs taken over the past 30 years.

Historical Introduction

In very early times Canterbury was a tiny settlement beside a ford over the River Stour, surrounded by low hills leading up to the downs which cover much of east Kent. Few remains of its earliest residents survive, but some Bronze Age finds are evidence of at least sporadic occupation. The first real evidence of continuous occupation is from the Iron Age – the important fort at Bigbury, just to the west of Harbledown, and the remains of early houses which lie well under the present occupation layers of the city.

1. Canterbury seems never to have had any very ancient defences except the Bigbury Hill Fort just to its west in Harbledown parish, which is still to a considerable extent complete, though gravel extraction has destroyed some of its features. It consists of two separate enclosures, the smaller one having possibly been a cattle enclosure, joined to each other and surrounded by ditch and bank defences, made probably by or before about 100 B.C. and probably somewhat strengthened by the invading Belgae not long before the Roman incursions. It is normally covered by undergrowth, bushes and scrub, but this view shows it during clearance, when the shape of the whole fort was for a short time revealed.

The Romans built their town beside the river ford near the point where a salt water inlet from the sea met the river. They made their settlement into a great military, commercial and social centre for east Kent, their lifeline to the continent. Their great road, the Watling Street, which was largely based on a prehistoric track, led from London to Canterbury, where it branched into others which communicated with Lympne, Dover, Richborough and Reculver, bringing their great fortresses there, the *Classis Britannica*, their navy, and their villas and living communities in communication with each other and with Canterbury. To this centre people living in the rural areas could come for social and cultural activities, and government officials and soldiers could all pass through, travelling on good Roman roads to and from destinations all over the empire.

Much of the foundations of this great Roman town of Canterbury has been discovered over the years, some of it during the course of small building operations, but particularly during large scale excavations after the ruins caused by the 1939-45 aerial bombings had been cleared away but before extensive new developments had commenced. From these excavations we know that the Roman town was surrounded by a great wall with entrance gates, that there were well-built gravel roads, fine houses with mosaic and tessellated floors and courtyards, baths and a large theatre. Canterbury was an administrative, cultural and leisure centre for the whole area, largely safeguarded from the seaborne incursions of northern tribes by its situation and by the Roman fleet and the great forts of the Saxon shore.

The inhabitants of the Canterbury area managed to maintain their established way of life until about the middle of the fifth century in spite of waning Roman authority, but from that time onwards Canterbury became a Saxon town. In about A.D. 488 Oisc, a Saxon, became king of Kent and made Canterbury his capital, establishing a royal dynasty which lasted until Wihtred's sons died in about A.D. 762. Probably the most famous of the royal family was Ethelberht, who became king of Kent in A.D. 560 and Bretwalda of other kingdoms northwards to the Humber. He was a pagan, but married the Christian princess, daughter of King Chariberht of Paris. She was accompanied by Bishop Liudhard when she came to Canterbury and her husband gave her an old Roman Christian church in which to worship. This was outside the old Roman walls, and is thought to have been the predecessor of old St Martin's, just to the east of the city.

A period of tremendous change was ushered in by the arrival of Augustine and his band of monks, charged with the mission of re-introducing Christianity to the country. This period is recorded, partly by established dates and facts, and partly by the writings of such men as Bede and Edmer, who lived centuries after many of the events they chronicled. Their work therefore consisted partly of recorded history and partly of recorded folk memory and oral tradition handed down through several or many generations.

However, it is certain that King Ethelberht gave Augustine a building within Roman walls which he restored and made his base church. This was the ancient forerunner of the present great cathedral and its traditional site was on ground now covered by the eastern end of the nave. The king also gave Augustine a piece of land outside the city walls to the east, to provide suitable accommodation for the burial of Christian kings and archbishops, burials not then being made within the areas where people lived. This was the origin of St Augustine's Abbey. Building went ahead and the abbey church was consecrated, followed by the chapel to the east of it, dedicated to Our Lady, five years later in A.D. 618. The Chapel of St Pancras, still further east, was also built at this time, or perhaps a little earlier.

Thus by the end of the second decade of the seventh century part of the Saxon cathedral within the walls was in full use, and St Augustine the first archbishop, and King Ethelberht and his queen, Bertha, were all dead and buried in the new abbey outside the city walls.

From this time onwards Kent, with Canterbury as its capital, developed in the more stable conditions then prevailing, keeping in touch with the continent, and developing its own culture. Kentish craftsmen worked with gold, silver and precious stones, and a small army of masons and woodworkers prospered from the erection of great new religious buildings, as did merchants exporting Kentish products and importing luxury goods which included glassware and precious stones.

During the next two centuries Canterbury became an important centre of learning and the two great religious houses, the abbey and the priory, became famous. In the last third of the seventh century the first great English school of learning was founded at the abbey under Abbot Adrian and the Priory School attracted scholars studying the classical curriculum. A keen rivalry developed between the two institutions, with the great abbey,

2.   This pile of rubbish marks the place where St Augustine, who died in A.D. 605 seven years after coming to England, was first buried. His body, together with those of several other early archbishops, was transferred, or 'translated', to a new site in the great new Norman abbey church which was begun in the time of Abbot Scotland (1070-87). This act was celebrated for many years by the 'Feast of the Translation of St Augustine' and each year on that day a great fair was held near the abbey gate, all the profits naturally being claimed by the abbot. The fair was eventually discontinued in the 13th century. It has been stated that at the dissolution of the abbey in 1538 the shrine and body of St Augustine was moved to the church of Chilham, on the Canterbury to Ashford road, and for many years a late medieval sarcophagus there was said to contain his remains, but when it was opened in 1948 it was found to be empty.

filled with monks regular, asserting its authority over the priory, under a prior and monks who did not conform to the regular discipline. The quarrels were frequent, bitter, and often petty and demeaning, but they continued for centuries.

Archbishop Theodore (668-692) installed the first organ in England in the cathedral and in about 760 a later archbishop, Cuthbert, built the baptistry, dedicated to St John, on the east end of the building. A few years later there was a period of political confusion when the Oisc Kentish dynasty died out and the county came under threat from Offa. After the Battle of Otford, the kingdom of Kent was absorbed into Mercia and, 50 years later, into Wessex, though Canterbury, classed as a borough, remained a place of importance.

The city suffered severely from Danish marauders, being attacked, overrun and plundered in 842 and again in 865 when the Danes were bought off but they continued plundering after accepting their tribute. In the tenth century the two great institutions re-commenced their building operations. Archbishop Odo (961-988) carried out work on the priory buildings and rebuilt the cathedral church, increasing the height of the walls and fitting a new roof, a project which took five years to complete. Abbot Dunstan enlarged the abbey church, re-dedicating it to St Peter and St Paul, and St Augustine.

The city was again the target for invading marauders, this time Thorkill and his Vikings in 1011, when 7,000 people were said to have been murdered, the cathedral partly burnt, and Archbishop Alphege taken prisoner. The abbey however was untouched, probably because the abbot came to terms with Thorkill, Archbishop Alphege having refused to pay protection money or permit a ransom to be paid for him. In consequence he was murdered by his captors in one of their drunken brawls. King Canute, in an act of restitution for his own terrible behaviour, brought St Alphege's body back to Canterbury and repaired the cathedral in 1023. It was in this repaired building that Edward the Confessor was crowned in A.D. 1043. Not to be outdone, Abbot Wulfric began major works at the abbey church, in 1049, demolishing its eastern end and the western end of Our Lady's church. In the space created between the two buildings he began his great new work, the Rotunda, the lower part of which still survives.

After the Battle of Hastings William I marched along the coast to take Dover, and then passed to Canterbury where he stayed a month and built his earthen motte and bailey castle outside the city walls. This castle, destroyed in the 19th century by the building of the railway, was not for the defence of the city but for the protection of his own garrison, a constant warning to the local people not to oppose him.

In the following year the Saxon cathedral was destroyed by fire and soon afterwards the last Saxon archbishop, Stigand, was deprived of his post, to be succeeded by Lanfranc in 1070. He, confronted by the embers of the old Saxon cathedral, and by a totally inadequate priory, cleared the whole site, and rebuilt in the Norman style, introducing to the priory the strict Benedictine rule for the monks. He also founded two hospices, St John the Baptist in Northgate for the aged, sick and poor, and St Nicholas at Harbledown for lepers. These were the first of a number of hospices established in and near the city in later centuries.

Abbot Scotland (1070-1087) followed suit and set about rebuilding the old Saxon Abbey church. He cleared away almost all the old buildings and erected on the site a great church. By his death he had finished all but the western end of the nave, this being completed by his successor, Abbot Wido. In this great new building the remains of St Augustine and several other early archbishops, and King Ethelberht and his queen, were ceremonially re-interred.

3. This stone, let into the turf to the west of his Rotunda which was never finished, records the grave of Abbot Wulfric who, in about 1050, commenced a great rebuilding project which was abandoned when he died in 1059.

More extensive written records survive from the 11th century, the most important being Domesday Book of A.D. 1086. It illustrated how acquisitive the religious institutions of Canterbury had already become, the Archbishop holding Sandwich and 25 manors, St Augustine's Abbey 30, and Christ Church Priory monks 23. These holdings were to increase both in number and in value throughout the medieval period.

Early in the 12th century Archbishop Ernulf rebuilt the Saxon crypt and Lanfranc's choir, which was completed by Conrad and dedicated in the presence of King Henry I and King David of Scotland. The campanile or bell tower, a separate tower to the south of the cathedral, contained five bells which were given by Prior Conrad and a sixth was given by Prior Wibert in the 1160s. This campanile was eventually destroyed in an earthquake many years later.

In the middle or second half of the 12th century the great stone castle, the ruins of whose great square keep still survive, was built to the south-west of the enclosed area within the city walls. This castle was quite separate from the early motte and bailey constructed immediately after the Norman landing, and was most probably built by Henry II, the great stone castle builder of the 12th century.

Certainly up to the middle of the 12th century the abbey retained a certain dominance over the priory and this continued until, in 1170, Archbishop Becket was murdered in the cathedral and, following his canonisation and the public penance of King Henry II, the great surge of pilgrimages began. These increased year by year, pilgrims flooding in from all over the country and from Europe. It was a heaven-sent opportunity for the religious houses. The whole city became pilgrim orientated, and the provision of living accommodation and food, together with souvenirs and trinkets sold to the vast numbers coming to Becket's shrine, brought much prosperity, both to the city itself and to the surrounding area. Canterbury's two weekly market days became sufficient to supply the many visitors from the country districts round about.

Of the many hospices catering for the pilgrims perhaps the most famous of all was the Chequer of the Hope on the corner of Mercery Lane, mentioned in Chaucer's *Canterbury Tales*, but most found accommodation in much more modest places, many sleeping rough. At first these pilgrims came from deeply religious motives, to visit Becket's shrine, to worship in his cathedral, and to be shown the precious relics of the saint. Later they came to escape from the monotony of a constricted medieval life, for a leisurely journey of pleasure in the company of kindred spirits, and for the opportunity to see something of the country or of the world. But whatever their motives, pilgrims brought three centuries of profit to the city and, indeed, to the country villages and manors which were often hard put to provide sufficent food for the multitude.

In 1174 disaster struck the cathedral. A terrible fire destroyed Conrad's 'Glorious Choir' and its rebuilding was commenced by a great master mason, William of Sens. As the result of falling from the scaffolding when the work was barely half-finished, he went home on a stretcher, a cripple, and the work was completed by another great mason, William the Englishman, who went on to complete the eastern transepts, the Trinity chapel and the great corona. These works still survive today, a magnificent memorial to a very great craftsman. In 1220, 50 years after Archbishop Becket's death, his body was transferred, or 'translated', with great ceremony, to William the Englishman's new Trinity chapel, where an elaborate shrine had been prepared.

In 1216 the Dauphin of France, in league with some dissident English barons, invaded east Kent and took possession of Canterbury and its great stone castle. There is no account of any battle, so it is probable that the city and its defences were surrendered, perhaps because the authorities were in sympathy with the invaders who, soon after an unsuccessful siege of Dover Castle and the death of King John, withdrew to France.

At this time too the Dominican and Franciscan Friars established themselves in the city, but the White or Augustinian Friars did not arrive until early in the following century. At their first coming, the friars were warmly received but their popularity waned greatly in later medieval times.

In 1283 Abbot Thomas Fyndon commenced a new building programme in St Augustine's Abbey. This included new kitchens, an abbot's chapel, and the great entrance gateway which still survives, though the upper part has been somewhat modified and of course the damage sustained during the bombing in the 1939-45 war has been repaired. At the same time, over at the cathedral, Eastry carried out many repairs to the choir and installed new stalls and a wooden screen. The bell tower, too, was provided with 11 new bells. The fortunes of the religious establishments were at their peak in the 13th century. The priory had a full complement of monks regular, the cathedral was thronged with pilgrims, and St Augustine's Abbey also shared in the great influx of visitors of all social backgrounds. The friars shared in this prosperity and undertook new building work, while the ordinary people of the city also prospered in modest degree from the pilgrimages.

4. The choir is one of the greatest surviving examples of early medieval building. It was begun by William of Sens and completed by William the Englishman, who was also responsible for the Corona at the far end. The original photograph was probably taken *c*.1900; this illustration is a copy of a postcard dated 1904.

In 1289 King Edward I was ceremoniously entertained at the abbey by the abbot, and 10 years later he was married in the cathedral to Margaret of France. To the religious authorities it must indeed have seemed a golden age. The pilgrims came in ever increasing numbers, contributing both to the institutions and their altars and to the civil business of the city. Gifts and bequests of money and land, even whole manors, poured in year by year.

This golden age was suddenly brought to an end by disease. Epidemics of varying severity were always a feature of medieval life and most of them were local or short lived, but not so the Black Death which in 1349 brought widespread death and disaster in its train. It also brought the reality of sudden death which threw a mantle of deep gloom over all human activities for several decades. In 1376 the city witnessed a sad cavalcade as the remains of the Black Prince were carried through the streets to burial in the cathedral, and it was a time of peril as well as of mourning since the French at that time were in the ascendant and were threatening armed raids and even full-scale invasion. Archbishop Sudbury organised the rebuilding of much of the perimeter walls, and the old Westgate with its church on top was demolished as a weak point in the city defences and the present Westgate was erected. A new church, dedicated like the old one, Holy Cross, was built beside the new gate.

Troubles never come singly and in 1382 an earthquake brought down the old bell tower, a building separate from the main part of the cathedral to the south-east, and caused damage to the cathedral itself and to parts of the priory. Yet in spite of everything, between 1381 and 1414 the priory cloisters were rebuilt, the old nave was demolished and the present magnificent nave was erected by the greatest builder of his time, the king's master mason, Henry Yevelle. At the abbey Thomas Ickham built the Cemetery Gate which still survives. There was also, at this time, a detached campanile or bell tower to the south-east of the great abbey church.

By the early years of the 15th century it was said that there were as many as 100,000 pilgrims each year making the journey to Canterbury, yet by the middle of that same century the numbers began to decline rapidly and consistently. The great age of faith, and of the religious life, had passed and the power and authority of the church was beginning to wane, while at the same time a new increasingly powerful middle class of educated laymen was rising to prominence.

In 1448 Canterbury received a charter giving it a mayor and in 1461 another charter granted it county status. The result was that the power of the church over the civil affairs of the city was almost destroyed and, although some matters were still at least influenced by the church, it would never regain its earlier dominance.

In 1470 St George's Gate at the south-east end of St George's Street was built, but St Augustine's Abbey was in a parlous financial state, its incomes much reduced, pilgrim numbers falling dramatically, many of its buildings in a poor state and its detached bell tower in ruins. In the same year the Great Festival, which had been held every 50 years since Becket's death, was so badly supported that permission was given for it to be repeated the following year. The situation at the priory and cathedral was, however, more stable. The Bell Harry Tower, which replaced the old Angel Steeple, was completed in 1500 and the last important piece of building carried out before the dissolution was the erection of the Christ Church Gate in 1517, three years before the final great 50-year festival took place in 1520.

In 1536 the suppression of the old religious institutions began all over the country, though a gradual but terminal decline had set in many years previously. Even the famous priory at Canterbury was reduced to one-third of its previous complement of monks, and St Augustine's Abbey had only 30 monks inhabitating its vast buildings. The friaries and other smaller houses were even harder hit. They had all long since ceased to be the holy, charitable and caring institutions they once were, and had become self-indulgent, closed, privileged communities, concentrating their efforts and resources on endless legislation, on the business of running their enormous holdings of land, and on the preservation and expansion of their considerable rights and privileges. Their day was done. To the people of Canterbury their passing was of no particular moment. The one great source of profit to them, the annual pilgrimages and the 50-year festivals, had dwindled and the people resented the monks' continuing exactions and interference in civil affairs. Moreover, Canterbury was a proud royal borough and possessed valued 15th-century charters which gave the city its own mayor and county status.

The small religious houses were simply 'invited' to surrender to the Crown, and this seems to have been done in Canterbury by their few remaining members without difficulty, the dispossessed friars and other religious being absolved from their vows and dispersed. The priory and the abbey however were large institutions with much property, and still with a number of inmates. The abbey was surrendered on 30 July 1538 by Abbot John Essex and his 30 surviving monks. All were granted pensions, the abbot receiving 200 marks a year (a mark being worth two-thirds of a pound so by the standards of the time he became very well-to-do indeed, though he did not live very long to enjoy it). Each of his monks received 100 shillings a year, about the amount a parish priest would earn at that time.

The empty abbey property was vested in the Crown, and Henry VIII lost no time in putting it to use. He had a king's lodging built there, using the abbot's residence and much material salvaged from the old buildings. It was becoming usual to have such king's lodgings, which were comfortable safe houses, on routes used by royalty and other very important personages, each about a day's ride from the next. This king's lodging, which incorporated Fyndon's Gate, the main entrance to the old abbey, was matched by another at Rochester, and some of the material, including roofing lead, was sent there from Canterbury. Much of the material from the old monastic buildings all over east Kent was re-used to build forts and harbour defences, and Kentish ragstone was sent from St Augustine's to strengthen the defences of Calais. From that time onwards loads of stone and other building materials were sold on the site to anyone willing to come and collect it, and one can only speculate on how many treasures must have found their way illegally into private hands.

The King's House was handed over to the hated Cardinal Pole by Queen Mary, and later Queen Elizabeth I granted it to Lord Cobham. It subsequently passed through other hands, parts of it even becoming a pleasure park, inn and brewhouse before it was bought in 1844 and converted into a missionary college. It remains an educational institution to this very day.

The situation of Christ Church Priory and the cathedral was quite different. It was not until 20 March 1540 that the prior and his 24 surviving monks surrendered to Henry who, in April 1541, granted it to the 'New Foundation'. According to Hasted this was to consist of 'a dean, twelve prebendaries, six preachers (nominated by the archbishop), six minor-canons, six substitutes, twelve lay-clerks or singing men, one of whom is organist, a master of the choristers which are in number ten, a chapter clerk, two masters of the grammar school, fifty scholars, twelve almsmen (nominated by the Crown), two vergers, two vestry keepers, with other inferior officers, as bell ringers etc.'. The old prior, Thomas Goldwell, and the monks were well looked after, being given pensions and offered posts in the New Foundation or in other churches, which most of them accepted, though Goldwell and several others preferred to retire to a secular life. Parts of the old priory buildings were converted to provide houses for the dean and prebendaries, and other parts were demolished.

The years of Queen Mary's reign were sad ones for the people of Canterbury. She and her archbishop Cardinal Pole attempted to re-establish the old religion, and even those who supported these attempts must have been revolted at the terrible religious persecution which cast such a blot on this cruel woman's reign. Many victims were imprisoned for months in the cold, damp and insanitary undercroft of the old stone castle where numbers of them died from disease and starvation, while those who survived were publicly burnt to death on pyres on the site which is now marked by the stone obelisk of the Martyr's Memorial inscribed with the names of 41 victims who died there. These disgraceful and distressing scenes were brought to an end by the death of both the cruel queen and her henchman Pole within a few hours of each other. The whole country welcomed the great queen, Elizabeth I, the monarch who established the foundations of modern England.

She inherited a country terribly divided in its religious and civil loyalties, and with abject poverty among the citizens of both towns and countryside. Canterbury was no exception. The income from the pilgrimages had ceased altogether since the 1530s and the city no longer enjoyed the substantial trade the pilgrims once brought. Though the number of state and business travellers was increasing, they in no way filled the gap. The cloth trade, one of the city's industries, was very depressed, and the threat of war between England and the Roman Catholic countries of the continent, particularly France and Spain, was a further disincentive to trade, so much so that Parliament was forced to take steps to deal with the poverty of many towns, including Canterbury.

One important measure, adopted in 1557, was the encouragement of the immigration of Flemish weavers from the Low Countries. Many of these employed local dyers and other families were engaged in one or other of the various crafts associated with the weaving industry. After the severe religious persecution in Antwerp in 1576 large numbers of Walloons brought their skills and settled in Canterbury alongside the native and Flemish weavers, to produce a boom in woven cloths which continued for many years. Their principal speciality was 'bays', a somewhat coarser variant of the old traditional Kentish Broadcloth, woven on a wider loom. Some of the old decaying buildings of the dissolved religious bodies were used as woollen factories, in particular the Blackfriars, the refectory there becoming a weavers' hall.

Queen Elizabeth gave permission for these newcomers to use part of the crypt of the cathedral for them to worship in their own tradition, and this privilege is still exercised. She herself visited Canterbury during her perambulation of Kent in 1573, staying in the King's House which her father had built in the ruins of old St Augustine's Abbey. She was entertained by the mayor and the city fathers, and by Archbishop Parker, who during his tenure of office rebuilt the Archbishop's Palace.

The many periods of acute anxiety caused by the threat of foreign invasion during her reign culminated in the Armada crisis in 1588, the passing of which was welcomed by the people of Canterbury and in particular her newer citizens, the refugees from continental religious persecution. This period also saw the development of paper manufacture and the growth of the city as an administrative, trade and business centre for the surrounding area.

In the 17th century tension between Crown and people flared up again, the arbitrary behaviour of the Stuart kings provoking hostility over many matters. Sir John Finch, elected M.P. for Canterbury in 1614 and again in 1625, was made Speaker of the House in 1628, and though very pro-royalist at first, even he was forced to oppose the king later on many matters. In June 1625 Charles I was in Canterbury waiting for the arrival at Dover of his 15-year-old bride to be, Henrietta Maria. They were married in the cathedral and afterwards the marriage was consummated at the King's House. During the Civil War the loyalties of the people of the city were divided. The clergy were solidly pro-royalist, as were many of the gentry, but other members of the gentry, the mayor and councillors, and most of the ordinary people supported Parliament. A Parliamentary force entered Canterbury and were 'received by the mayor and sherrifs with acclamation, took two loads of arms and six barrels of gunpowder from the dean and prebendaries and some plate from a papist, Mr. West'. They also did much damage to the interior of the cathedral. In 1647 Canterbury people rioted against the Parliamentary edict that there should be no observance of Christmas Day, the disorder lasting almost the whole week. Disaffection with some of the Parliamentary excesses provoked disorder on several occasions, and royalist groups took the opportunity to seize control of Canterbury, but they surrendered to Parliament's forces under Ireton in June 1648, and though there were threats of further trouble, none of any moment occurred.

King Charles II returned to the country in 1660, accompanied by his brother (who later

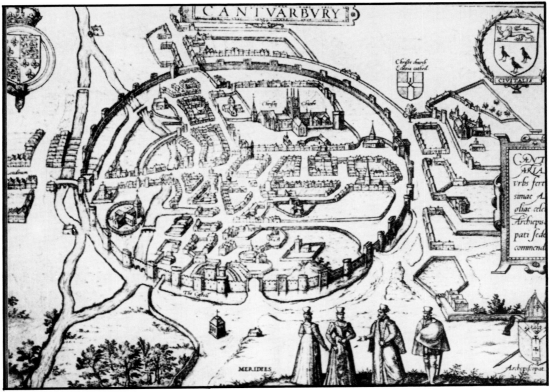

5. This fine old map, attributed to G. Hoefnagel, is thought to have dated from about 1570 and has become a source of great interest and discussion. It shows the city, still principally confined within its ancient walls, the cathedral and its environs, and a water-filled moat to the south-west. The Westgate and its bridge (to the left of the map) are well illustrated, as are a number of churches and other buildings unfortunately no longer in existence.

became King James II) and, after landing in Dover, rode to Canterbury to be welcomed by the civic authorities and churchmen before occupying the King's House and then moving on towards London. During the reign of King James II, much alarm was felt in Canterbury by the refugees because of frequent rumours of royal intentions to re-introduce Roman Catholicism. There was much relief everywhere when James fled the country in 1688.

During the 17th century the weaving of woollen cloth in the city declined because of competition from continental sources and from 1622 there was great distress among the cloth weavers, who never regained their earlier level of prosperity. The weaving of silk, however, prospered. Silk weaving in Canterbury was being carried out in 1571, and by 1665 it was recorded that there were 126 master weavers in the city employing over 2,000 people. The zenith of this silk weaving industry was in the period following the revocation of the Edict of Nantes in 1685, when many refugees set up their looms in Canterbury, as previous skilled refugees had done before them. By 1710, however, the number of looms was reduced to 334, and by the end of the century only 10 were left. Many efforts were made subsequently to revive silk weaving on a modest scale, but it proved impossible. Another craft, the building and operation of corn mills powered by the waterwheels

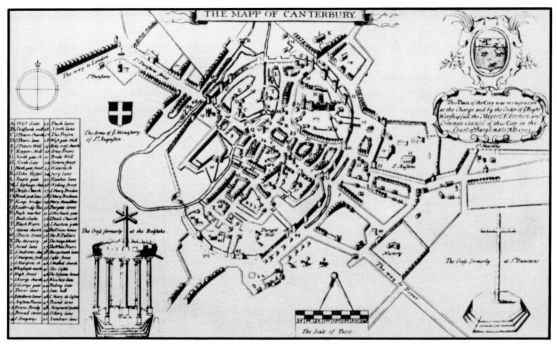

6. A print of an old map of the city. The dedication in the top right-hand corner states: 'This plan of ye city was re engraven at the charge and by the order of ye Right Worshipfull the Mayor, Aldermen and Common Council in the Court of Burghmote 1703'. Among many interesting features, it shows two crosses, one 'The Cross formerly at St Dunstans', and the other, 'The Cross formerly at the Bulstake'. This bullstake was situated in the Buttermarket just outside the cathedral gate.

utilising the waters of the River Stour, showed considerable improvement in this period when the old undershot wheels gave way to the more powerful breast variety.

In the 18th century the city underwent a period of great change. The declining silk industry revived considerably before finally coming to an end beaten by what Defoe, writing in the 1820s, called the introduction of 'printed calicoes and chints etc.'. The decline of silk weaving was matched by a sudden new prosperity brought about by the planting of thousands of acres of hops all round the city, and the market for hops, corn and other general farm products, brought in from the surrounding rural areas, grew substantially. The expansion of business and trade, and the stationing of large numbers of soldiers later in the century, brought a considerable increase in the number of substantial houses for business and professional men and army officers, the bricks for which came from local kilns. Large quantities of 'deals', that is wood for building, came in by sea to Fordwich, as did the coal to heat the big new houses, while 'oyl, wine, grocery etc.' was shipped from London to Whitstable and thence to the city.

As business expanded travel became increasingly important and large numbers of horses were stabled in Canterbury to pull coaches, traps and wagons to connect the towns of east Kent with London. The roads radiating from the city were almost all turnpiked in the 18th century, that from the city to London (the Watling Street) in 1730, to Whitstable in 1736, to Chilham and on to Charing in 1762, to Ramsgate in 1787, to Barham, completing the link to Dover and to Folkestone, in 1781, and to Sandwich in 1802. The new Dover Road, from St George's Gate southwards, was cut in 1790, and by the beginning of the 19th century only the Westgate survived of the ancient gateways which once pierced the city walls. The city made a big stride into the modern world by the establishment of the Commission for Paving, Lighting, and Watching the Streets, which held its first meeting in 1787.

Besides the development of trade and business, the city became a fashionable place in which to live, being a cathedral city with good communications with the outside world and with a thriving social life. Members of the old ruling classes, successful businessmen, and army officers built large houses for their families in Canterbury. This of course favoured the rise of nonconformity, which had already made considerable inroads into the religious life, and places of worship sprang up to serve a variety of different sects, many of which failed to survive though others, such as the Baptists and the Methodists, prospered.

A notable event, emphasising the growing concern with the large numbers of poor people in the community, was the establishment in Longport of the Kent and Canterbury Hospital in 1791, thus bringing the possibility of skilled medical treatment within the reach of all.

The 19th century began in farce and ended in anxiety. It is recorded that in 1801 the mayor of the city, and the commandant of the military garrison, were at loggerheads, a major bone of contention being the sentries posted at St George's Gate, which led from St George's Street to the New Dover Road. The mayor requested the removal of these sentries because he claimed that they were rude to females passing through the gate, but the commandant refused point blank to remove his men, whereupon the mayor had the gateway demolished. How much fact, and how much fiction there is in this story, is uncertain. The maintenance of law and order was a problem at this time and in the first decade of the century the city built the Sessions House in Longport, near their new hospital and, a few yards further up the hill, the 'County Gaol and House of Correction'.

Although the 1801 census revealed that Canterbury was no longer the largest town in Kent, its population of a little over 9,500 having been overtaken by that of Chatham with 1,000 more, commercial and professional life prospered. It was a busy city, the fulcrum of east Kent's religious, commercial, professional and social life. It was also an unhygienic place, with narrow, claustrophobic streets, little dwellings housing large and often multiple families, a limited water supply, no adequate sewage or rubbish disposal systems, with rough road surfaces, often a sea of mud in wet weather and of dust in dry, fouled with the droppings of hundreds of horses which were used, and stabled, in the city, providing the sole means of transport. There was of course no gas nor electricity, and smoke from hundreds of chimneys poured into the atmosphere. There was also no control of workshops, stables or businesses, nor over the watermills which obstructed the free flow of the river water, causing extensive floods in wet and stormy periods. Many horse-drawn stage coaches left the city each day for London and for the principal towns of Kent and through coaches halted to pick up or set down passengers. Heavy wagons, pulled by teams of horses, plodded through the narrow streets, sometimes blocking them completely for periods, to the great annoyance of residents and travellers alike. Alehouses abounded and drunkenness and crime was a constant and an increasing headache for the civic authorities.

Yet it was also a city which experienced a great religious revival, no less than 17 substantial churches and chapels being built in the 19th century, and this number does not include the use of small halls and even rooms in houses for a number of sects of ephemeral status and limited survival. The principal nonconformist churches however were very successful and do still flourish.

There were several markets to supply the needs of Canterbury and a fine new building was erected in 1828 to serve as the corn exchange. The watermills ground large quantities of corn and the flour they produced was carted away in large horse-drawn covered wagons to places many miles away as well as supplying local needs.

But from the end of the first quarter of the century onwards enormous legal, administrative, social and transport developments which were to change, not only the city itself, but also the life styles and occupations of its residents, took place. Many local government acts provided for the improvement of streets, adequate water, gas and sewage supplies, together with the establishment of a professional law enforcement system.

The coming of the railway age was heralded by the development of harbour facilities at Whitstable and the building of the pioneer steam railway between these and Canterbury, which was opened in 1830. Passengers and goods could now be transported to Whitstable by rail, and then up river to London by a hoy which sailed every other day. This line was followed by the Ashford, Canterbury West and Ramsgate line in 1846, the Sittingbourne to Canterbury in 1860, its extension to Dover in 1861, and the lovely little Elham Valley line from Shorncliffe to Barham in 1887, which was extended to the city in 1889. In consequence the stage coach network and most of the old, slow goods wagon traffic died, and horse-drawn vehicles became increasingly limited to feeding the railway stations with goods and passengers which previously went all the way by road. Hundreds of men previously engaged in horse-drawn transport were thrown out of work, only to be very slowly absorbed, if at all, in the newer occupations.

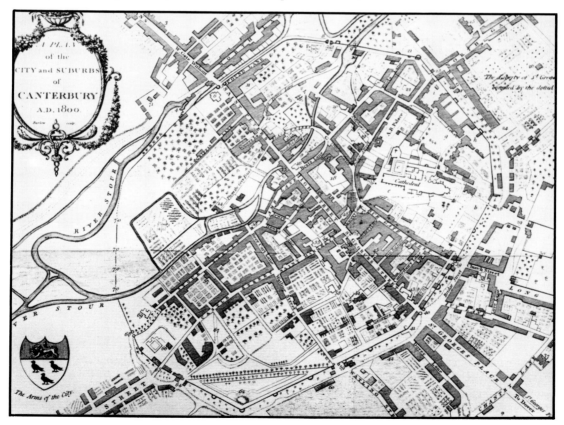

7a. (*facing page*) The central area of a map of *c*.1800 labelled 'Barlow Sculp'. Barlow worked at the turn of the century and this map shows the city before the coming of the railways or the internal combustion engine. The city was an important centre during the stage coach era, and saw many heavy and slow goods wagons, drawn mostly by bullocks, travel through. The map was used in Hasted's *History of Kent*.

REFERENCES,

To the City and Suburbs.

1.	St Dunstans Church	37. Doges Chantry
2.	County Goal	38. St Pauls Church
3.	Jews Synagogue	39. Burgate
4.	Cock Mill	40. St Georges Gate
5.	Westgate	41. Cattle Market
6.	Holy Cross Westgate Ch.	42. Bridgers Alms Houses
7.	Deans Mill	43. St Georges Church
8.	Postern	44. White Friers
9.	New Bridge	45. Shambles
10.	Abbots Mill	46. { St Mary Magdalen, Burgate Church
11.	Canterbury Wells	47. Butter Market
12.	St Peters Church	48. The Old Chequer Inn
13.	Cogans Hospital	49. Town Hall
14.	Grey Friers	50. St Mary Bredman Church
15.	Kings Bridge Hosp. & Mill	51. Assembly Rooms
16.	All Saints Church	52. Corn Market
17.	Theatre	53. St Andrews Church
18.	Dancing School Yard	54. Fish Market
19.	St Alphage Church	55. St Margarets Church
20.	Black Friers	56. { Poor Priests Hospital, the City Work House
21.	St Radigunds Baths	
22.	Borough of Staplegate	57. Maynards Spital
23.	Northgate & Church	58. { St Mary Bredin, or Little Lady Church
24.	Northgate Burial Ground	
25.	St Johns Hospital	59. Riding Gate
26.	St Thomas's Chap. Ruins	60. Rodeaus Town
27.	Jesus or Boys Hospital	61. The Dungeon House
28.	Church Postern	62. The Dungeon Field & Hill
29.	Lady Wottons Green	63. Hams Alms Houses
30.	Ethelberts Tower	64. Wincheap Gate
31.	County Hospital	65. Worthgate
32.	St Pancrace Chapel	66. Castle & County Sessions H.
33.	St Martins Church	67. Chapel Church Yard
34.	Smiths Alms Houses	68. Postern
35.	Barton House	69. St Mildreds Church
36.	St Pauls Burial Ground	

70. Breaches in the City Wall.

71. Westgate Court.

7b. The reference panel which occupies a corner of the 'Barlow Sculp' map. Many of the buildings listed here no longer exist and this makes both it and the map of particular interest.

8. One of the 'Union' coaches run by Richard Chitty and Robert Fagg and Co., which plied between London, Canterbury and Dover to carry passengers between London and Paris. It picked up passengers, and set them down, at Canterbury's old Guildhall, situated on the corner of the High Street and Guildhall Street. Passengers to and from Sandwich and Deal travelled via Dover, and this picture shows one of these feeder services bound for Dover before setting off for Canterbury and Holborn, where their London service terminated. These 'Union' coaches provided a service to and from London three times a day, each taking two full days to cover the distance. There were a number of these coaches serving Canterbury, all of them dwarfed by the Chaplin firm which provided a network of services covering the south-east region of the country.

9. This beautifully restored coach used to run on the London, Canterbury and Dover service and is now to be seen in the covered yard of the *Royal Victoria and Bull Hotel*, a wonderfully kept old coaching inn at Dartford. This coach carries the Royal Arms on its side, since it was a Royal Mail coach and as such had priority at all the toll-gates and other possible obstructions on the road.

In the second half of the century in particular there was a spate of house building, some large houses for business and professional men, and for those of independent means who began to take up residence in cathedral cities, but most of all for artisans and small businessmen, for whom modest little houses were erected in narrow streets interposed between the main streets of the city, and also in the rapidly expanding suburbs outside the old city boundary.

Canterbury again became an important garrison town in 1873 when the Buffs Regimental Depot was established, and many local soldiers fought in the Boer War, a great memorial later being built in the Dane John Gardens in memory of those who fell in that campaign.

10. One of the London, Chatham and Dover Railway Company's locomotives heads a passenger train eastwards round the south of the city. The cathedral is shown as viewed from the south-west, and a windmill is also to be seen in the background, to the left of the locomotive's funnel.

One can but wonder what future generations will think of our own stormy 20th century. It started with the Boer War which was the curtain raiser for the terrible Great War of 1914-18 which robbed Canterbury, and the whole country, of its generation of young men and of much of its treasure. The 1939-45 war left a permanent mark on Canterbury through the dreadful air raids, especially those of 1942, which destroyed so much of the southern part of the city and many of its ancient buildings, but fortunately left the cathedral comparatively unscathed, though its library was destroyed.

Perhaps time will mellow subsequent rebuilding. The loss of the old Guildhall was a serious and almost certainly avoidable disaster, and many of the new premises are, to be charitable, not exactly prepossessing. There were, however, unnecessary acts, such as the intrusion of the ugly roof of the new Marlowe Theatre upon what was a memorable view over the city to the west end of the cathedral. One also grieves at the loss of small businesses which give any town, and especially a cathedral city, its individuality and so much of its charm. The triumph of the chain store is, however, a national problem.

As the railway superseded the old horse-drawn stage coaches, so modern road transport has largely superseded the railway, and now modern pilgrims to this beautiful city, literally in their millions, flood its narrow streets, its surviving ancient buildings acting as a continuing magnet for all.

Introduction

11.   Looking west from the principal gateway of old St Augustine's Monastery one sees a panorama of much of Canterbury's eventful past. The medieval walls are built upon Roman foundations, Lady Wootton's Green in the foreground was the path by which Bertha, Christian Queen of the pagan King Ethelberht of Kent, passed with her bishop, Liudhard, to worship at the tiny church of St Martin, while in the background is the great cathedral, the nearest part being the beautiful Corona built by master mason William the Englishman and, towering over all, is the magnificent Bell Harry Tower, the last great medieval addition to the city's skyline. It all contrasts strangely with the modern traffic lights and car park notices.

The Arms of the City.

Barlow sculp

12.   The arms of the city, the Archbishop, and the Dean and Chapter, used by Hasted in his great work *A History of Kent c.*1800.

13.   Canterbury and its environs as depicted on Symonson's map of 1596.

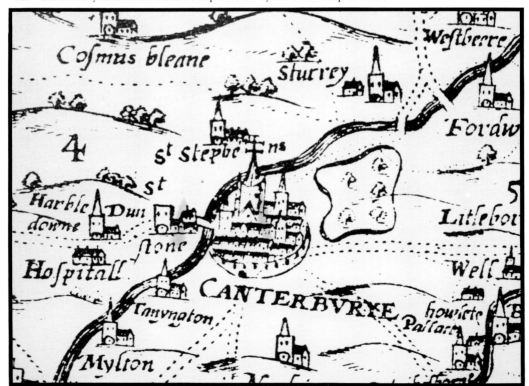

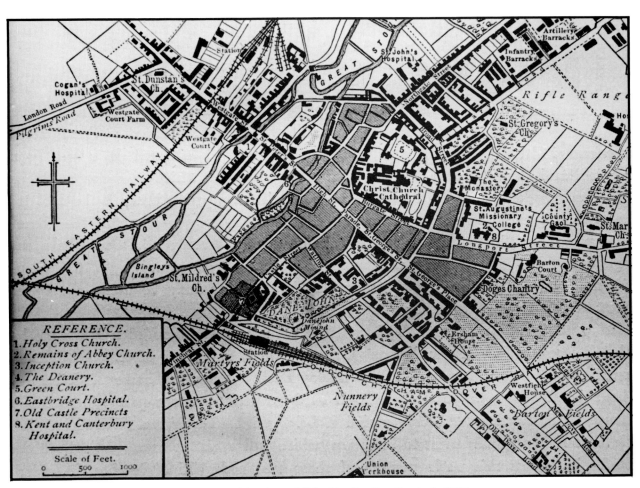

REFERENCE.
1. Holy Cross Church.
2. Remains of Abbey Church.
3. Inception Church.
4. The Deanery.
5. Green Court.
6. Eastbridge Hospital.
7. Old Castle Precincts
8. Kent and Canterbury
   Hospital.

Scale of Feet.
0   500   1000

14.   A map of the city published in *Our Own Country* in 1882.

Views Across the City

15.   Though pilgrims and other travellers did catch occasional glimpses of the city as they walked from London, this was the first really comprehensive view of Canterbury they would see, having breasted the last hill up past the old Leper Hospital at Harbledown (the old Herble Down because of the variety of herbs which grew there). It is still a fine viewpoint, even though so much development has taken place in the intervening years. The view of the west end of the cathedral is particularly fine. This view was drawn by Geo. Shepherd, engraved by H. Adlard and published by Geo. Virtue in 1828.

16. This fine old etching, used by Hasted in his *History of Kent*, is dated 1799 and is labelled: 'South View of the City of Canterbury. M. Thomas delt. T. Medland sculp'. The cathedral is shown to the left of centre, and St Augustine's Abbey to the right of centre. The fields shown here reaching up to the city boundary are now covered by more recent development. The horse and the covered two-wheeled cart in the foreground is very typical of many which at that time brought produce from local farms and market gardens into the city daily.

17. This view of Canterbury from the north-east, *c.*1800, shows green fields stretching right up to the inner part of the old city boundary. The impact of this view is much less dramatic today because of the large number of taller buildings which have since been erected, obscuring much of the cathedral from view.

St Augustine's Abbey

18.   Looking westwards over the remains of the great nave of St Augustine's Abbey, built by Abbot Scotland but completed by his successor, Abbot Wigo, in 1901. Abbot Scotland's church was the fifth church built on the abbey site. The first was the abbey church of St Peter and St Paul consecrated in 613, St Mary's to the east followed in about 618 and, further still to the east, St Pancras, about the same date. The little known chapel to the west of the abbey church, now almost completely lost, was of the first half of the 11th century, and the beginnings of a major church, the Octagon, partly built by Abbot Wulfric in about 1050, was never completed and was almost razed, like the other earlier buildings except St Pancras, by Abbot Scotland for his great, and the last, abbey church.

19. The Saxon church at St Augustine's Abbey had side chapels where very important people were buried, kings in the south chapel, and archbishops in the north chapel which is shown here. Much subsequent rebuilding and the final destruction after the 1538 dissolution has destroyed almost all traces of these chapels except this small portion of the north chapel of St Gregory, now covered by a roof to protect the sites of the graves of three early archbishops, Laurence, Mellitus and Justus. These three sites carry modern stone tablets indicating where each one was buried. That for Mellitus for instance records the following: 'ST. MELLITUS, CONSECRATED FIRST BISHOP OF THE EAST SAXONS 604. THIRD ARCHBISHOP OF CANTERBURY 619-624'.

20. The pillars and stone arches shown here were originally at the north side of Abbot Scotland's great nave. After the dissolution, Henry VIII had a royal posting house built here, using the north side of the nave and part of the abbot's quarters beyond it, and the Tudor brick topping the arches is plainly visible. He stayed here on several occasions on journeys between London and Dover, but Queen Mary presented it to the infamous Cardinal Pole, and later Queen Elizabeth handed it over to Lord Cobham. In 1625 it housed Charles I, on the night when he met Henrietta Maria on her way to join him from France, and in 1660 Charles II stayed there on his way back to London at the Restoration. The mass of material at the extreme left is what remains of the base of Ethelbert's Tower, one of the two towers which stood at the western corners of the great nave.

21. (*left*) This gateway, simpler than the main gateway at the other end of Monastery Street, nevertheless has some details in common with it, notably the octagonal corner towers topped by simple octagonal turrets with battlements. A curious feature is the decorated machicolations. The main purpose of this entrance was to give access to the cemetery inside which was used for interments by the general public and not by the inmates of the abbey. However, that cemetery has long since been closed, and in the middle of the 18th century the gateway was converted into a dwelling. Some of its early records survive. It was erected by order of Thomas Ickham, the sacrist of the abbey, in the later part of the 14th century at a cost of £466 13s. 4d.

22. (*below*) Now restored after bomb damage in the 1939-45 war, the great gateway, often known as the Fyndon Gateway after the abbot during whose tenure it was built, was erected in the first decade of the 14th century in the Decorated Gothic style. The decoration is exuberant – the octagonal front corner towers are plain at their lower level, but higher up enriched with crocketed triangles and ogee curves, culminating in ribbed octagonal turrets, crowned with embattlements. The entrance gateway spans the whole space between the corner pillars, so providing ample room for the passage of carriages. This gateway is now the entrance to the buildings erected to the design of the Victorian architect, William Butterfield, for his client, Beresford Hope, for the St Augustine's College in 1844. It is now used by the King's School, and is sadly not open to the public. This engraving was published by S. Hooper in 1784.

23. An 18th-century view from inside the great gate of St Augustine's Abbey. The foreground was later covered by the buildings of the missionary college designed by William Butterfield following the purchase of this part of the ruins by A. J. B. Beresford Hope in 1844. This purchase included the *Old Palace Inn* and the brewery which then occupied the buildings round, and including, the great gateway.

24. The staging house behind the archway provided casual accommodation for Henry VIII and for Queen Elizabeth in her perambulation of Kent in 1573. There King Charles I consummated his wedding after the ceremony in the cathedral and in 1660 Charles II and his brother stayed briefly on their way to London. After passing through a number of hands, however, it became a brewery and public house, and the Great Court inside was used for variety shows, dancing, and as a beer garden. Then it was bought and reconditioned when the missionary college was established there by Royal Charter granted in 1848. This engraving of St Augustine's Gate by H. Adlard was published by Geo. Virtue in 1828.

25.   The chapel of St Pancras, shown on the extreme right in this 1784 drawing, was the easternmost of the abbey buildings and was a small Saxon chapel with a rectangular nave and an apsidal chancel. It was probably built in the early seventh century and is similar to the Saxon chapels at Reculver, and Bradwell in Essex. The nave was separated from the chancel by three semi-circular arches carried by the walls and two intermediate pillars. The building was constructed of re-used Roman bricks, and these were laid in regular courses. There were later alterations and additions, in particular a porticus to the north, west, and south walls and, in the 15th century, a new chancel of rectangular plan, a large east window and a new roof.

26.   On the extreme right of this 1784 view is the ruin of Abbot Scotland's great nave, and the semi-ruin of St Ethelbert's Tower, while in between them is the Bell Harry Tower of the cathedral. On the left is the Cemetery Gate and, to its right, the tower of St Paul's church. On the extreme left is the tower and spire of another of the city's churches, though which one is uncertain.

27.   This fine print is entitled: 'West view of Ethelbert's Tower, St. Augustine's, Published Jan. 21 1801 by
W. Bristow, M. Thomas Del. R. Pollard Sculp'. This great tower stood at the north-west corner of Abbot Scotland's
nave which was completed in the last decade of the 12th century, and was one of the finest examples of late Norman
architecture in the country. Said to be unsafe, it was demolished in 1822.

28. Another view over the city which later development has obscured. The great cathedral broods over the remains of St Augustine's Abbey in the foreground. There is a very formal stone-edged pond in this area even today, but its age is uncertain. This picture was drawn by Geo. Shepherd, engraved by J. Rolph, and published by Geo. Virtue in 1828.

29. After the dissolution of the monasteries, this piece of land, then known as Mulberry Tree Green, was no longer kept in good condition, the people of St Paul's parish using it for all kinds of village activities. There was also an alehouse, which may have been the old Chequer mentioned in the 1788 description of the boundaries of the Borough of Longport, and none of this greatly pleased the Lady Wootton who owned some of the old monastic property nearby in the mid-17th century. In consequence, in spite of opposition from the people of the parish, she fenced the green off and forbade access to it. Her enclosing fences have, of course, long since gone and it has again become an open space forming a suitable approach to Abbot Fyndon's great entrance gate shown at the left of the picture.

Friaries

30. All traces of the Austin or White Friars have disappeared but this plaque, in a passageway off the main street, records the site on which their buildings were erected after their arrival in the city in 1325.

31. This photograph, which is undated but appears to be of the early 1930s, is of the remains of the Greyfriars' Friary. In 1224 a group of nine Grey Friars landed at Dover and walked to Canterbury where they divided up. Four went on to London and five stayed in the city, living for a time at the Poor Priest's Hospice whose master, Alexander of Gloucester, gave them land behind the hospice and built there a modest chapel for them. This became the order's first house in the country. In 1267 John Digge of Canterbury gave them some land adjoining this on which an extensive Friary was built. It was dissolved in 1538 and passed into the hands of private owners. The buildings suffered severely from enemy action in the 1939-45 war and few of them survive much above ground level. The little building, shown on the left, was built across the branch of the river Stour which flows through the city a few yards up river from the King's Bridge. The building shown has been reconditioned and part of it now serves as a small chapel. Most of the ground is used as a market garden.

32.   When the house of the Grey Friars was built in the 13th century, on an island in the river Stour to the south-west of the King's Bridge, ways had to be made to reach it. One was by means of a lane from St Peter's Street, and another was by the building of a wooden bridge across the river in 1264. The brick and stone bridge shown here was built in 1309. Permission to build it was granted on condition that boats could pass beneath it. This was made possible by a large arch in the centre. Later rebuilding and repair have preserved the arch to this day.

33.   In the 1230s, 20 Dominican or Black Friars settled in Canterbury on land just to the north of the present High Street and St Peter's Street. Modern roads such as The Friars and Blackfriars Street indicate its position. In its heyday the friary possessed a cloister, round which were the usual conventual buildings, in this case a large church with a long nave and choir without aisles, a chapter house, a refectory and, just over the river, the guest hall. In its early years this friary received many valuable bequests, some from the royal house. Following the dissolution it remained deserted for some years in royal hands, but later passed through a number of private hands and most of the old buildings were gradually cleared away. The illustration shows one of the two major surviving parts, the refectory, built on the east side of the river, halfway along Blackfriars Street. In the last four centuries it has been used as a woollen factory, a weavers' hall, a store, a church for Baptists, Unitarians and Methodists in turn, and later for the Christian Scientists.

34. This fine old mid-18th-century engraving shows, on the right, the refectory which still survives. On the left are the three arches of the Blackfriars' bridge and the footbridge which connected the refectory with the guest hall on the opposite side of the river. This guest hall also survives and can now be seen behind the Marlowe Theatre.

35. A drawing of the main entrance to the Blackfriars Friary, made shortly before it was demolished in 1787. It consisted of squared flints and stone dressings with a horizontal band of carved stone halfway up the front surface, above which were recesses for figures of saints. It stood at the junction of The Friars with St Peter's Street. The Black Friars settled in the city in 1236 but the friary was closed in December 1538.

The Cathedral

36. In the 19th century many beautiful illustrations such as this were reproduced in various publications. This one was used in *Cathedrals, Abbeys and Churches*, published in 1891.

37. After passing through the subdued light of the Christ Church Gate the modern pilgrim is suddenly confronted with this fine view of the cathedral. On the right is the Bell Harry Tower, on the left the twin west towers and, between them, with its towering clerestorey and flying buttresses, is Henry Yevelle's 14th-century Perpendicular Gothic nave, one of the greatest of that master mason's achievements. The porch at the base of the nearest west tower is the principal entrance, though the great west doors between the towers are opened for processions and distinguished guests.

38. The south-east exterior of the cathedral exhibits contrasting styles of building. On the right is the 12th-century south-east transept and, just to its left, a fine small tower of the same period, part of the Norman-style building which was consecrated in A.D. 1130. On the extreme left is the southern wall of the south transept with its enormous Perpendicular Gothic window of about the year 1400, and great buttresses extending the full height of the walls and terminating in delicately carved finials. The small pale coloured, newly refaced chapel at the bottom centre is the Chapel of St Michael, now known as the Warriors' chapel, noteworthy for its fine collection of tombs and memorials.

39. This view of the cathedral and its surroundings from the top of the Westgate suffers from the intrusion of the unnecessarily ugly roof of the Marlowe Theatre.

40.· Unusual and often unexpected views of the cathedral can be obtained from many situations. This one was photographed from the upper window of premises in Burgate Street.

41. 'A drawing of the Cathedral Baptistry' by J. Godfrey, *c*.1780.

42. Wibert's tenure of office as prior (1151-67) was a period of extensive development of the priory buildings. He built this famous Norman staircase, and also the infirmary chapel, some accommodation for poor pilgrims and the treasury. This illustration dates from *c*.1900.

43. The ruins of the priory infirmary in 1891. These are still in much the same condition and are to be seen immediately to the north-east of the cathedral's eastern end.

44. The cathedral in the second half of the 18th century. Unless considerable artistic licence was employed, the precincts must have undergone much change soon after this drawing was produced.

45. This illustration, published in *Our Own Country* and in *Cathedrals, Abbeys and Churches*, among other 19th-century books, is entitled 'The Place of the Martyrdom in the Cathedral'.

46. This illustration, from a postcard of *c.*1910, is of the Archbishop's Palace, which was rebuilt by Archbishop Temple in 1896 on the original medieval site, using what old material was available from the old building.

47. This illustration of the Christ Church Gate, used in *Our Own Country*, shows its condition in 1882. It was the principal entrance to Christ Church Priory and was built between 1517 and 1521, chiefly of Kentish ragstone, though some brick was also used at the sides. It was the final addition to the great priory before the dissolution which occurred only a few years later. It was late Perpendicular Gothic in style, square in plan with octagonal corner towers and carried on its front face many fine heraldic devices on stone shields. Its great wooden doors were embellished with the arms of Juxon, Archbishop of Canterbury 1660-63. Gostling wrote that the gateway was restored in 1803, Portland stone being used. However, having weathered very badly in the early years of the 20th century to the state shown here, it was restored by Caroe in 1932, some artificial stone being used on that occasion. It was noted that 'The two turrets which used to stand at the front corners were demolished in the nineteenth century at the request of a banker in the High Street so that he might see the cathedral clock without hindrance'. They have, of course, since been replaced.

48. The reconditioned Christ Church Gateway. It will be noted that the top corner turrets have indeed been replaced, having been dedicated and unveiled in 1937 by the Bishop of Chichester. They were constructed of Clipsham stone. This gateway must be one of the most frequently photographed and drawn of any subjects in the city, and it is certainly a very fitting entrance to the cathedral.

49. The south-west porch of the cathedral nave which forms the main entrance to the building was commenced in A.D. 1425 and completed two years later. A major renewal of the stonework was carried out in 1862 and it has been refurbished again recently. It is a beautiful example of the Perpendicular Gothic style, its complex decoration contrasting wonderfully with the simple crisp vertical lines of the south aisle of the great nave.

50. The choir, high altar and corona of Canterbury Cathedral, from *Cathedrals, Abbeys and Churches*, published in 1891.

51. In Canterbury the ugly multi-storey car park does little to enhance the interest of the city, yet from its top fine views over the city can be obtained. This is one of them, a telephoto view of the cathedral from the south. The functional, box-like shape of the modern buildings in the foreground contrasts strangely with the Gothic splendour of the great medieval cathedral behind them.

2. This very detailed view of the cathedral dates from 1654. It will be noticed that at the west end (extreme left) the earmost (north-west) tower has a spire and four small corner pinnacles, unlike the south-west tower which has four corner innacles only. The reason is that although Lanfranc's late 11th-century nave survived until it was rebuilt in the erpendicular Gothic style between 1378 and 1405, the two original Norman west towers remained in their original ondition until the south-west one was rebuilt between 1424 and 1434.

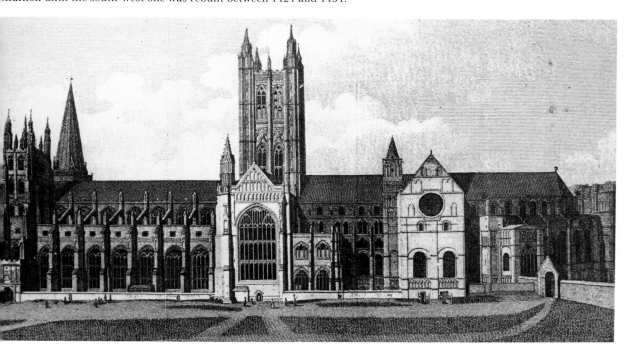

53. This view of the cathedral from the north-west was drawn by H. Gastineau, engraved by H. Adlard, and published in 1828 by Geo. Virtue. By this time, though the old Norman tower remained at the north-west corner of the nave, the spire and the corner pinnacles had been removed, probably because of decay in the wooden framework or deterioration in the lead sheathing, giving the tower an unfinished appearance.

54. Published in *Our Own Country* in 1882, this picture shows the west end of the cathedral as we see it today. In 1832 the old Norman north-west tower was in poor condition and it was decided not to repair it. Consequently, it was demolished and the present tower was built as a copy of its twin at the south-west corner. Though the constructional and decorative details are similar, there is a very marked difference in the colour of the stone between the two, which reveals unmistakably their difference in age.

Churches

55. St Martin's is a famous and ancient little building standing on a hillside a little to the east of the city, now unfortunately hemmed in by large trees planted by the Victorians. This view can no longer be photographed. It is said to be the little church which the pagan king of Kent, Ethelberht, gave to his Christian queen Bertha for her devotions. St Augustine is also said to have preached here. It is certainly one of the very early Christian churches in the country and is mentioned by the Venerable Bede. It consists of a very early long chancel, a nave, and a Perpendicular Gothic west tower, with a vestry built in 1845 at the north-west corner of the nave. The building contains much early work, including a great deal of Roman brick and Saxon walling, thought to date from the seventh century. The south sides of the chancel and nave, in particular, reveal extensive areas of Roman brick, but experts are uncertain as to whether it is part of an earlier Roman building, or whether the Saxons re-used Roman material. A very striking feature of the interior is the fine, probably early Norman, or possibly late Saxon, tub font.

56. St Mildred's church, situated at the south-west end of the city near the old castle keep, is certainly a surprise, since first appearance suggests that it is a middle to late medieval building much rebuilt and restored in Victorian times, but closer inspection reveals that this was a substantial Saxon pre-Conquest building consisting of a long nave and chancel, to which was added a 13th-century north chapel, a 15th-century north aisle (over which was a tower demolished in 1832) and a south chapel built in 1512 with a flat roof and diaper work in the walls. Much of the south and west walls survive from the old pre-Conquest church, including great stone corner quoins. The building has many interesting features, notably crown post roofs with substantial tie beams, a fireplace in the south chapel and a good collection of hatchments.

57. The massive quoin stones at the south-west corner of the nave of St Mildred's church. These stones, arranged here in 'long and short' work, are good indicators of early building, Saxon builders having used this technique extensively.

58. St Peter's is a very typical town church, situated just off the busy St Peter's Street. It started life as a small, very simple building probably of the 11th century. To this was added a plain and slender west tower around the time of the Conquest, a quantity of salvaged Roman material being re-used in its walls. It now consists of a nave and chancel with full-length north and south aisles terminating in triple gable ends and includes work of the 11th to the 14th centuries. St Peter's originally had a roodloft, its opening surviving above the south arcade. The space left by its removal, and that of the chancel arch, together with its wide aisles under crown post roofs, has given the church a surprisingly spacious interior.

59. An early view of St Stephen's church, Hackington, drawn by H. Gastineau in the 1820s. It was used in Ireland's *History of Kent*.

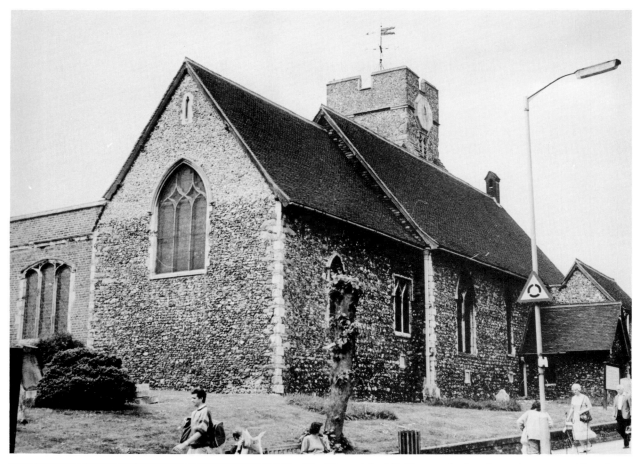

60. The original St Dunstan's church, on the corner of London Road and the A290 to Whitstable, was a late Saxon or early Norman church. Many additions were made in the 13th and 14th centuries and it was largely rebuilt in the 15th century. It has a simple slender Perpendicular Gothic west tower, a nave and chancel with aisles to both, the eastern one of which is the chapel of St Nicholas, used as the chapel of the Roper family. Their family house is nearby, behind the surviving Roper gateway. It was in the Roper chapel that Margaret Roper interred the head of her father, Sir Thomas More, in a leaden casket after his execution in 1535.

61. This tower, still standing in Burgate Street, is all that remains of the ancient church of St Mary Magdalene which once stood on the site. This late Perpendicular Gothic tower, built in 1502, stood at the western end of the north aisle. The aisle was linked with the nave and chancel by four Gothic arches which sprang from slender octagonal pillars and square capitals. There were a number of monuments, several of which, including that to John Whitfield who died in 1691, are preserved inside the surviving tower. This church was demolished in 1871, much of the material including the pillars and arches being used to extend the sister church of St George the Martyr in St George's Street which was itself destroyed in the enemy bombing of the city in the 1939-45 war.

62. The tower of St George the Martyr, still standing in St George's Street, is all that remains of the church following aerial bombing in the 1939-45 war. The church contained work of the Norman and Gothic periods and had an octagonal font in which Christopher Marlowe, the dramatist who was born and brought up in this parish, was baptised in 1564. In the vestry was a painting of Guy Fawkes, of Gunpowder Plot notoriety, with the date 1632 and the inscription: 'In petuam Papistarum Infamiam'. In the 1870s the building was much changed. A new chancel was built and a north aisle added, the arches and pillars from the old dismantled church of St Mary Magdalene in Burgate Street being re-used, that parish having been united with St George's.

CHRISTOPHER MARLOWE
Dramatist
BAPTISED IN THIS CHURCH
26TH FEBRUARY 1564
DIED AT DEPTFORD
30TH MAY 1593

63. On the side of the old tower of St George's church is this plaque commemorating the baptism there of Christopher Marlowe. His father, a Canterbury shoemaker, lived in St George's parish and was very active in local affairs. Christopher went to King's School and then to Cambridge after which, in about 1586, he lived a wild life in London, becoming involved in the city's underworld, engaging in some secret service work, and writing the great plays for which he has since become famous, proving himself to have been the greatest of all of Shakespeare's predecessors, probably influencing his work. Marlowe crammed much into the seven furious years he spent in London before he was murdered in a brawl in Deptford, though the suspicion remains that he may have been silenced because he came to know too much through his secret service activities.

64. This 'D-shaped' bastion, in a surviving section of the city wall opposite Lower Bridge Street, has been roofed in and extended on its inner side to create the Zoar chapel, dated 1845, of the Strict and Particular Baptists.

65. The Roman Catholic Church of St Thomas sits on a piece of land bordered by Burgate Street and Canterbury Lane. Not considered of any special architectural distinction, it was designed by a local architect, J. G. Hall, built in 1874/5 and extended in 1962.

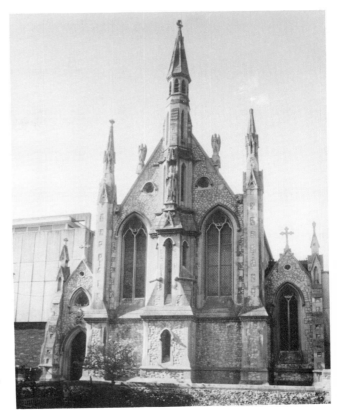

66. This modern United Reformed church in Watling Street, a pleasing brick building, is unfortunately overpowered by the massive multi-storey car park immediately behind it. The church was erected during the large-scale rebuilding of this part of the city following the extensive destruction caused by enemy air raids in the 1939-45 war.

Hospices & Hospitals

67.   This Victorian view of the interior of the gatehouse of the Hospice of St John the Baptist shows the timber framing of the structure, and two top-hatted residents in the entrance passageway. This hospital, said to be one of the oldest in the country, was established by Lanfranc (archbishop 1070-1089) as one of two, the other being the leper hospital of St Nicholas at Harbledown. For many years they were administered jointly. St John's was built to house poor and infirm men and women apart, Lanfranc being adamant on this point. Not only were the sexes housed in separate accommodation, but even the chapel had two naves for the same purpose. A disastrous fire destroyed the old Norman chapel, and many other buildings too, in the 14th century. The present chapel seems to have been built a few years after that disaster. The early 16th-century gatehouse shown gives access to the interior, which consists of a central lawn surrounded by the accommodation for the inmates, the chapel and a refectory. The living quarters were brought up to date in 1960, and they still provide accommodation for needy people today.

68. The Swan is a fine old 16th-century building adjoining the entrance gate of St John the Baptist of Northgate, the ancient hospital of which it is still a part. Today the Swan is leased out for private use to help to provide income for the hospital.

69. The Hospital of St Thomas the Martyr Upon Eastbridge, often abbreviated to Eastbridge Hospital, was built by Edward FitzOdbold in the later years of the 12th century to provide short term accommodation for poor travellers and pilgrims. A few years after its foundation, William Cokyn's Hospital of St Nicholas and St Katherine in Peter Street was amalgamated with it, and William left all his possessions to the combined institution when he died. The hospital prospered as a result of gifts and legacies, and though it passed through difficult times, notably in the 14th and 16th centuries from financial irregularities and seizures, it still survives to provide accommodation for the brothers and sisters who live there. This view, of part of the buildings spanning the river, can only be seen from a boat which can be hired by the Weavers on the opposite side of the street. Though the residents' quarters are private, the remainder of the building, including the two chapels, the crypt, and the refectory with its mural and numerous exhibits are open to the public.

70. This ancient timber-framed building forms the entrance to the Hospital of St Nicholas at Harbledown, set up in the 1080s by Lanfranc as the second of his two foundations. This hospital was for lepers and when, after the Middle Ages, leprosy had declined, it became a home for the sick and needy and, finally, a sheltered home for the elderly, in which capacity it still functions.

71. This fine old church of the Hospital of St Nicholas at Harbledown dates from the end of the 11th century though the north aisle is a century later, and some of the detail work is of the 14th and 15th centuries. It has some fine medieval stained glass in its east window, ancient wooden pews, a wooden tower ladder and the old arches spring from unusual carved capitals.

72. The Black Prince's Well at Harbledown was in earlier times famed for the medicinal qualities of its water. The well was fed by a spring issuing from the side of a hill below St Nicholas's Hospital which used to supply its water. The Black Prince is said to have drunk water from the well during the course of his travels to and from France.

73. This section of ancient wall, on the south-west side of the Old Dover Road, is almost all that remains of the Hospital of St Lawrence (in old records sometimes spelt Laurence) founded in 1137 by Abbot Hugh of St Augustine's Abbey, though the name is perpetuated in Canterbury's famous cricket ground. The hospital used to accommodate monks who had contracted leprosy. It may not always have been a male-only establishment since, Hasted records, in the reign of Henry II Richard de Marci granted the tithes of his lands of Dodingale 'to the hospital of St Laurence ... to the intent, that the brothers and sisters of it should have these tithes ... trusting that they would remember him and his in their prayers'.

74. On the banks of the river Stour, in Stour Street, stands the Poor Priests' Hospital on a site continously occupied for centuries. According to recent excavations an important stone domestic house was built here between 1175 and 1180 by Lambin Frese, the Canterbury moneyer. In 1220 the premises were made into a hospital 'for the relief of the poor and indigente priests' and soon afterwards, in 1224, gave shelter to the first Grey Friars to come to England under Archdeacon Simon Langton, the patron of the hospital. It was rebuilt in 1373, but all through the medieval period it remained extremely poor, never having attracted the rich patrons so many other such institutions enjoyed. It survived the dissolution but was surrendered to the Crown in May 1575 and three months later was handed over to the city of Canterbury who used it first as a gaol and later as a workhouse. Later still it became a store, an organ works and then an infant welfare centre. In 1982 it was converted into a museum.

75. This plaque, on the front wall of the Poor Priests' Hospital, records two previous distinguished residents of the property. Adam of Charing was legal adviser to, and friend of, Archbishop Becket who, after a quarrel, excommunicated his old supporter. How long this excommunication lasted is not known, but Adam later founded the leper hospital of St Stephen and St Thomas at New Romney. This has long since ceased to exist.

76. The Jesus Hospital in Northgate was founded by Sir John Boys at the end of the 16th century, the deed poll being dated 1599, and it was planned for between 12 and 20 inmates, one-third of whom were to be females and unmarried. A school for 20 boys was part of the scheme and the warden was in charge of both the hospital and the school. Sums of money were set aside for clothing and for the boys of the school there were premiums payable when they secured apprenticeships to Canterbury employers. The school was closed in 1879 but the hospital, much rebuilt and improved in recent years, still survives as a valued charitable institution for the aged. Jesus Hospital, the most substantial surviving charitable hospital in Canterbury, is a two-storey block in brick with tiled roofs, and was enlarged by a southern addition in the same style in 1933.

77. This inscribed stone, embedded in the wall over the front entrance door of Jesus Hospital, records Sir John Boys's charitable act in founding the hospital in 1595. It was obviously the work of a mason of somewhat modest ability, far removed from that of the great stonemasons who were producing magnificently worked memorials in marble and alabaster.

SIR·IHON·BOYS
KNIGHT FOVND=
ED·THIS·HOSPIT=
ALL·ANNO·1595

78. William Somner recorded that a wealthy Canterbury citizen called Maynier the Rich, or Maynard, founded this hospital of Our Lady in the 12th century. It was enlarged at the beginning of the 17th century by Leonard Cotton, a prosperous Canterbury businessman who had been mayor of the city. From that time onwards it was known as Maynard and Cotton's Hospital. Following storm damage it was rebuilt in 1708 in a very simple manner as a continuous single-storey building in brick, with a tiled roof and decorative gables, the accommodation for each inmate consisting of a bed-sitting room, a kitchen and an outside toilet. Since the last war the rooms have been extensively modernised. A further extension was made in 1970 when Miss Phyllis Hooker paid for two extra units of accommodation as a memorial to her parents.

79. The John Smith almshouses, on the south side of the road to Sandwich opposite the prison, were built to accommodate four men and four women in separate apartments, but have recently been modified to provide only four units but with modern equipment and more room and comfort. They form a single-storey brick-built block with tall chimneys and a tiled roof with ornamental gable ends, the eastern gable showing the foundation date, 1657. This charitable foundation was the gift from John Smith and his wife in gratitude for the birth of a son after they had been married for 20 years and had long given up hope of producing a son and heir.

ON THIS SITE FOR 144 YEARS
BEFORE MOVING TO SOUTH CANTERBURY
HE GENERAL KENT & CANTERBURY HOSPITAL
UPPORTED BY VOLUNTARY CONTRIBUTIONS
STEADFASTLY SERVED THE SICK POOR
1793·1937

80. (*above*) This tablet, attached to railings in Longport near the present footpath to St Augustine's Abbey, records the site of the original Kent and Canterbury Hospital. The hospital cost just over £4,000, raised by voluntary subscriptions. It was opened in April 1793, treating both in- and out-patients. The need for a modern building led to its removal to Nackington Road.

81. (*right*) Early in the 19th century Nunnery Fields Hospital was erected by the city authorities as a workhouse, but it was later handed over to the Canterbury Group of Hospitals and is now devoted to geriatric care.

82. (*below*) The present Kent and Canterbury Hospital, in Nackington Road, is a modern, low, reinforced concrete building with a clock tower on the central wing facing the entrance. It was designed by Cecil Burns, the foundation stone was laid on 12 July 1935 and patients were moved in from the old hospital in Longport in September 1937.

83.   The T. S. and H. Cooper almshouses in Lower Chantry Lane were built in 1900. They consist of a single-storey block of brick and tile incorporating six separate living units, with an ornamental gable at each end. Each of the units has its own double pitched roof with the ridge running from back to front, each front terminating in an ornamental gable over a bay window. Four tall chimneys complete this curious layout. The Cooper family, well known in the district, built these almshouses for aged former employees.

84.   Hospitals and hospices do not only belong to the past. This photograph shows Her Majesty Queen Elizabeth the Queen Mother greeting voluntary workers at the opening ceremony of the Pilgrims' Hospice in Canterbury in June 1982.

Memorials

85.   The Dane John Hill was one of three modest mounds in the area, and a Canterbury alderman named Simmons
included it in his improvements to the gardens there in the later years of the 18th century. He created a terraced walk along
the inside of the city walls, planted a row of lime trees, and shaped and built up the mound to its present height, making
a pathway up its sides so that people could admire the view from the top. This old picture, drawn by Geo. Shepherd,
engraved by H. Adlard, and published by Geo. Virtue in 1828, shows the completed hill, and early 19th-century citizens
walking along the terraced path.

86. The Martyr's Memorial as it appeared *c*.1911, before the insensitive development of a housing estate in the area. This simple cross, set up in Martyr's Field, marks the place where 30 men and 11 women were burnt alive for their religious beliefs in the reign of Queen Mary. The name of each victim is incised into one of the faces of the square base.

87. This great obelisk, in the middle of the Dane John Gardens, is a memorial to 'the officers, non commissioned officers and men of the Buffs-East Kent Regiment and of the Imperial Yeomanry of East Kent who gave their lives in the country's cause during the war in South Africa 1899-1902'.

Canterbury Memorial to
THE REV. RICHARD HARRIS BARHAM.

R. H. BARHAM ("Little Tom Ingoldsby").
Aged 5 Years.

R. H. BARHAM.
Aged 50 Years.

September 25th,
1 9 3 0

With the Compliments of
The Mayor of Canterbury.

88. A card commemorating the unveiling of the memorial bronze to the Rev. Richard Harris. It shows him at the ages of five and fifty years.

89. Mr. Mead was the recipient of this card inviting him to be present at the unveiling of a memorial bronze to one of Canterbury's illustrious sons, Richard Harris Barham, the author of *The Ingoldsby Legends* who was born in Burgate Street. This memorial survives beside the entrance door of the art shop of Messrs. Crump and Bell on the corner of Burgate Street and Canterbury Lane, the place where he was born.

The Right Hon. Lord Northbourne
and The Right Worshipful the Mayor of Canterbury

Request the pleasure of the company of *H. T. Mead Esq.*

At the Unveiling of a Memorial Bronze to the Memory of
The Rev. Richard Harris Barham,

A Native of this City.   Author of "The Ingoldsby Legends."

The Ceremony will be performed by the
Very Reverend William Ralph Inge
K.C.V.O., LL.D., D.Litt., F.B.A., Dean of St. Paul's

On Thursday, the 25th of September, 1930.

The Assembly will meet in the Guildhall, Canterbury at 3 p.m.

Please reply if you are able to attend, to
THE RT. WORSHIPFUL THE MAYOR,
ST. NICHOLAS RECTORY, CANTERBURY.

TEA PROVIDED
AFTER THE CEREMONY.

90. (*above left*) A *c.*1912 photograph of the memorial to Christopher Marlowe in its original position in the Butter Market. It consisted of the figure of the muse standing on an elaborate pedestal, surrounded by a square of iron railings at the corners of which were globes on decorated shafts. The semi-naked female figure, however, occupying as it did the prominent site at the cathedral entrance, was disapproved of by the religious authorities and when a central location was needed for the war memorial, the opportunity was taken to remove the offending figure to a more remote site in the Dane John Gardens.

91. (*above right*) The Christopher Marlowe memorial in its present site in the Dane John Gardens.

92. The City of Canterbury War Memorial stands in the square outside the Christ Church Gate, the site of the old Butter Market and the Marlowe Memorial. Hasted records that a cross was built there as early as 1416 by John Coppin of Whitstaple and William Bigg of Canterbury.

Public Buildings

93. This fine old building, the Corn Market, stood at the corner of Butchery Lane and what is now called the Parade. It was built in the 17th century, the ground floor open for the market stalls, and the first floor which was supported on piles or pillars, serving as a granary. Over the gable end was a small open turret housing the market bell which signalled the opening and closing times of the market. Hasted, writing at the end of the 18th century, noted: 'It has not been made use of for many years as a market, that being held in the open street, on the side opposite to it. The lower part of this building is partly inclosed as a night watch house, and the rest or forepart of it, for the sale of fish, toll free; a few hucksters for greens, and such like commodities; on the spot where this building now stands, was formerly the town house, or guildhall of the city, with the prison adjoining to it, before the present one was built, being called at that time the Spech house'.

94. The Canterbury gaol was begun in 1806 and completed in 1810 to the design of George Byfield. The lintel over the stone entrance gateway is inscribed: 'COUNTY GAOL AND HOUSE OF CORRECTION', a description which accorded well with early 19th-century theories of the function of a prison. The building is still in use. The Sessions House next door, designed by the same architect, is a grim forbidding two-storey cube with facing of Portland stone, sash windows and a central entrance door flanked by two full-height Doric columns.

95. The Canterbury Historical Society was founded in the *Guildhall Tavern* in 1769 and, after a modest beginning, was re-established in 1825 as the Canterbury Philosophical and Literary Institution in purpose-built premises in Guildhall Street. After the Public Libraries Act had been passed in 1858, the Philosophical and Literary Institution was disbanded, the Corporation taking over its functions and properties. This building no longer exists.

96. The Beaney Institute, a late 19th-century building in the High Street, incorporating the Royal Museum, the public library and the Slater Art Gallery, was designed by the architect A. H. Campbell. It houses many treasures, including important archaeological finds, particularly of the Roman period and those discovered during extensive excavations carried out in the bombed parts of the city before they were redeveloped after the 1939-45 war. The Slater Art Gallery has some fine exhibits, including several paintings by Sidney Cooper, the Canterbury artist. This illustration is from a postcard dated 1908.

97. Canterbury's old guildhall was demolished after being damaged in the Second World War. It was built on Norman foundations and contained medieval and 18th-century work. It was probably built in about 1438 on a site associated with local government even earlier. The illustration shows its interior earlier in the present century. The site, on the corner of Guildhall Street and the High Street, is now occupied by a modern shoe shop.

98. The old Holy Cross church was the second church of that name, the first having been a chapel built over the old Westgate and destroyed when the old gate was demolished in 1380. This new building was then erected beside the new gate. It consisted of a nave with north and south aisles, a chancel, a tower at the south-west, and an unusual old roof. The Perpendicular Gothic interior was completed by the provision of a font with an octagonal basin and a tall and elaborate wooden cover. Both are now in the church of Minster in Thanet. The building suffered three Victorian restorations, in 1860, 1870 and 1895, during the course of which much of its medieval character was destroyed. It was declared redundant in 1973 and the city council converted the building for use as their new guildhall. It was opened as such by H.R.H. the Prince of Wales, in November 1978.

99. The Sidney Cooper Centre in St Peter's Street, a small building with a large Ionic-style doorcase, was the birthplace of Canterbury's famous artist, Sidney Cooper, C.V.O., R.A. He was born in 1803 and lived to be 99 years old, painting almost until he died, and specialising in local and country scenes. A small selection of his considerable output hangs in the art gallery of the Beaney Institute.

100. The centre of much of the city's cultural life, the Marlowe Theatre is shown in its new setting at The Friars, off St Peter's Street, having moved from earlier premises in St Margaret's Street. The building was formerly the Odeon cinema.

The Castle

101. This late 18th-century illustration of the keep was published in Hasted's *History of Kent*. The first castle in Canterbury was an earthen motte and bailey defensive work which survived until it was destroyed by the building of the railway in 1860. The great stone castle, the keep of which is shown here, was built in the reign of Henry II between 1166 and 1174. The keep comprised four storeys: the great hall was on the second floor, below which was a domestic area and a basement used originally for the storage of supplies for the garrison but later used as a prison. Entrance was gained through a forebuilding on the north-west side, only a few traces of which remain. All the masonry of the perimeter walls and the buildings round the bailey have disappeared.

102. The remains of the keep in 1980. The castle had an undistinguished history. It was surrendered to the Dauphin of France in 1216, was reported to be very dilapidated in 1336, and was taken by a group of men led by John Salos, on their way to meet up with Wat Tyler's men in the rising of 1381. Having become almost completely ruinous, it was sold into private hands in the reign of James I and much of the outer walling was demolished in about 1770. The old keep became part of the waterworks complex and was later used as a coal store for the nearby gasworks. More demolition in 1817 left it virtually a ruin, but what remains is now carefully conserved as a national monument.

Walls, Gates, Towers & Bastions

103. The Chapel Bastion, situated in the section of wall at Broad Street opposite Lady Wootton's Green, is one of the finest wall bastions now surviving. It preserves an old inverted keyhole gun port and a number of putlog holes. These are small square openings into which lengths of wood can be inserted, these then carrying scaffold boards or planks from which men can carry out repairs to the surface of the building. These old medieval walls were built on the remains of the Roman and Saxon walls, much of which survives in this area. The walls were pierced by gates and had defensive towers and 'D'-shaped bastions, of which this is one. Such walls were useful for barring entry to the city of undesirables, beggars and unauthorised traders, and also for discouraging small raiding parties, but they were not sufficient to withstand a full-scale invasion force, or a long siege, because of the impossibility of guarding adequately the considerable length of the wall, and because of its vulnerability to destruction in places by mining, a common medieval offensive tactic.

104. Early apertures in defensive walls were usually vertical or cross slits, for observation and for firing longbows and crossbows. From the middle of the 14th century onwards, however, guns and gunpowder became more and more important, both in offensive and defensive warfare, and so wall apertures came to be shaped like inverted keyholes. Inside, platforms made of stone slabs were fitted, the guns resting on the slabs with their barrels protruding through the circular part at the base of the ports. Many of these are still to be seen in Canterbury, particularly on the walls of the Westgate, and also in the surviving 'D'-shaped barbicans in the city walls.

105. This illustration shows how the inner side of the projecting bastion was enclosed to convert it into a small wall chapel. Note the roughly hewn quoin stones on the right-hand side of the picture and the flight of open stairs by which a platform on the top, enclosed by a parapet, could be reached.

106. This interesting illustration of arches in the city wall was published by S. Hooper in 1784. These arches carried the wall over the river just to the north of the old Abbot's Mill. Later they were demolished. It has been said that this provided materials for the widening of the King's Bridge at the western end of the High Street though, according to the plaque beside the bridge, the widening was done in 1769. Today St Radigund's Street is carried over the river on a very ordinary brick bridge, near to the site of the former arches.

107. The Tower House in Westgate Gardens covers the site of part of the old city walls, and one of its defensive towers was incorporated in the mid-19th-century building. Several well-known Canterbury citizens lived there including William Howard who owned the Chartham paper mill three miles up river. Later, it was occupied by the owner of the Canterbury leather tannery whose descendant Stephen, and his wife Catherine Williamson, presented the house and gardens to the city in 1936. The gardens themselves have been considerably developed since that time and are now one of the most attractive areas of the city. Catherine Williamson became the first woman mayor in 1938, serving in that capacity for two years. Since 1962 the house has been used as the mayor's parlour and it forms a dignified setting for civic occasions. On the north side of the Westgate is the Sudbury tower in Pound Lane, which has also been converted into a residence.

108. St George's Gate, an elegant structure built in 1470, was, according to Hasted, formerly called Newingate and, prior to that, Ote-hill gate. The large reservoirs which supplied water to the city were located in the upper part of the gate, which has now disappeared. The man at the door on the right-hand side of the picture is beneath a sign which reads: 'Knott. Peruke maker. Hair cutter'. The peruke was of course a wig.

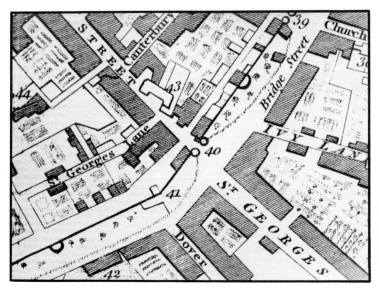

109. This is a small section of a map of 1800 published in Hasted's *History of Kent*, showing the St George's area of the city. The numbers indicate: 39. Burgate; 40. St George's gate; 41. the cattle market; 42. Bridgers Alms Houses; 43. St George's church; 44. the White Friars. This area was very heavily bombed in the 1939-45 war.

110. The Westgate was rebuilt by Archbishop Simon of Sudbury and completed in about 1380 and today is the only survivor of the city's many gates through its perimeter walls. The demolition of the old Westgate also involved the destruction of Holy Cross church which was built on and above the old gate. The new Westgate, said to be the work of the great Henry Yevelle, the king's master mason, was constructed of squared blocks of Kentish Ragstone, with many inverted keyhole gun ports. It consisted of two strong drum towers bridged by a recessed flat section, the lower part of which is perforated to form a passageway, which in early times could be closed by massive doors and a portcullis, the grooves for which still survive. In front was a drawbridge over the river Stour which ran immediately outside. Today Westgate houses a somewhat macabre museum of military exhibits, prison equipment and the old condemned cell, having served as the city gaol until 1829. From the top a fine view over the city can be obtained.

111. This engraving of Westgate from the north appeared in the second edition of Hasted's *History and topographical survey of the County of Kent*. It provides a stark contrast with the same view today, illustrating how much the area has changed in the last 200 years.

112. A print labelled: 'The West Gate, with part of Holy Cross Church, Canterbury. Engraved by George Cooke from a drawing by himself made November 1806'. On the left is the bridge over the river, and on the right an ancient building, now lost, between the river and Holy Cross church. Its site is now occupied by the flowerbeds beside the river.

113. This drawing of the Wincheap Gate, published in 1784 by S. Cooper, shows the gate shortly before its destruction. It appears to have always been a less impressive structure than the Westgate and St George's Gate, consisting of two modest square side towers bridged by a simple chamber over the doorway. It possessed no arrow slits, gun ports nor any other visible means of defence.

114. An 18th-century view of the medieval Riding Gate, used in earlier centuries for the carriage of manure and offal from the city. It was often reported as being in a ruinous condition and needing urgent repair. In 1799, while creating a public park for the people of the city at the Dane John Gardens, Alderman John Simmons demolished this old gate and replaced it with another.

115. Having demolished the medieval Riding Gate, Alderman Simmons built this simple gate in brick with a plain four-centre arch shown here in 1882 before its destruction in the following year. It was not replaced.

Mills & Bridges

116.   This 1771 illustration shows the Cock Mill as it was in about the middle of the 18th century. The mill seems to have had a simple, undershot water wheel, in which the wheel carries blades which just dip into the water and are activated only by the velocity of the water in the running stream, the most basic type of water wheel.

117. This 1772 illustration shows Holy Cross church, the Westgate and Cock Mill. The mill building, its water wheel, the boats on the millpond, and the backwater are all clearly drawn. In Domesday Book this mill is listed as belonging to the Archbishop. In the 13th century it was handed over by Archbishop Hubert to the Eastbridge hospital. Downstream, just beyond the Westgate, was another mill, once known as Shafford's, but by the end of the 18th century named after its current owner, Dean, who probably had it rebuilt. Later it was called Hooker's Mill, and it continued to work until it was burnt down some years ago and the site was cleared and laid out to provide a picturesque open riverside park.

118. This fine old drawing shows the old bridge over the river Stour at Blackfriars at the end of the 18th century, when its upper part was already ruinous, though the three arches were intact. It appears to have been a 13th-century construction.

119.   This view, down river from the King's Bridge, with the Weavers on the left of the bridge and the site of the old King's Mill on the right, shows one of the older parts of the city behind the modernised shopping streets. These tile-hung buildings line one stream of the Great Stour river, which divides into two just to the south-west of the city, the branch shown here passing through it, and the other flowing on to the north, outside the old walls and the Westgate, to rejoin the other a mile to the north-east. On the building to the right of the King's Bridge, a plaque records the site of the old King's Mill, in early times also referred to as Eastbridge or Kingsbridge Mill. Thorne's Chronicle states that King Stephen gave it to the Abbot of St Augustine's in exchange for the loan of 100 marks 'in his necessity'. Abbot Clarembald returned it to King Henry II in exchange for liberties granted to St Augustine's and he in turn granted it to Rohesia, the sister of Archbishop Thomas Becket, possibly as part atonement for Becket's murder. Hasted notes that later it was handed over to the citizens by King Henry III and they seem to have kept it and appointed a miller to run it for them.

120. A 1957 photograph of Barton Mill, half a mile down river from the Blackfriars, which in medieval times was held by Christ Church Priory. From the 12th century onwards the watermill in the manor of Barton stored the barley, ground it, and delivered the malt to the priory, where the brewhouse made beer for consumption by the monks. The Barton Mill was supervised by a senior monk who was called the Bartoner. Although malt was also bought from city maltsters from the 15th century onwards, it continued to be produced at the Barton Mill until the dissolution.

121. On the hill above St Martin's church stands St Martin's Mill, with a fine view over the city and the hills beyond. It was built in 1817 by John Adams and in its early years was called Buck Windmill. It seems to have worked continuously until 1890. It fell into decay in the early years of the 20th century and in 1920 was bought by a Mr. Cozens who, by the careful reconditioning of its stone tower and some additions, converted it into a private house. It is still well preserved. Its four sweeps have not of course been replaced, but the fantail, missing in a photograph taken before it was converted into a house, has since been replaced.

122. Abbot's Mill before its destruction by fire on 17 October 1933. It was never rebuilt. Its considerable size can be appreciated when it is compared with the houses beside it. Unfortunately there are few pictures of this mill just before its destruction and this one is damaged. The mill once belonged to the Abbey of St Augustine, having been bought by Abbot Hugh in the first half of the 12th century. After the dissolution it passed to the king and later to the city. In 1791 the business partnership of Messrs. Simmons and Royle leased it from the corporation and built a new mill on the site. This was designed by the famous late 18th-century engineer and specialist in water power, John Smeaton. His new mill was vast, being over 100 feet high, with stone and brick walls on the ground floor, white-painted weather-board above, and a slate roof. The two water wheels, each 16 feet in diameter and seven feet wide, provided power for cleaning the corn, milling, dressing and bagging the flour and working the crane which the six-floor height of the mill made essential.

Streets

123.   This fine old street, running parallel with the south-west boundary of the cathedral precincts, terminates at its lower end at the old Butter Market outside the Christ Church Gate. On the left of the illustration is the Liberty shop, for many years known to citizens and visitors alike as a very high quality baker's and tea shop. It is a fine and very solid medieval structure with a double overhang and a hipped tile roof, and its many details are well worth careful study.

124. Canterbury, always a great cathedral town, was also an important market town for the country round about. Livestock was brought to the cattle markets and geese, chicken, eggs, butter and vegetables to the Butter Market for sale to the city dwellers. The Butter Market, shown here, was also a place of meeting where residents watched, and sometimes took part in, activities as diverse as country dancing and bull baiting. The *Antiques of Canterbury*, published by William Somner in 1640, contains a map in which the 'Bull stake' is shown standing in the centre of the Butter Market. Canterbury War Memorial has replaced the old bull stake, but there is no memorial to the old mayor who, centuries ago, was beheaded there.

125. St Dunstan Street in 1911, looking towards the Westgate. On the left is the ancient *Falstaff Inn*, showing the very fine wrought-iron sign bracket which unfortunately had to be shortened later because it was constantly being damaged by high vehicles.

126. A fine drawing by Geo. Shepherd of Church Street in 1828. On the right is St Paul's Without the Walls, and in the distance is the cemetery gate of the old St Augustine's Abbey. From its assorted load, the horse-drawn wagon was obviously operated by one of many local carriers who served both the general public and the shops, since few of the little town shops at that time had their own transport.

127. Church Street, which leads from Burgate to the cemetery gate of St Augustine's Abbey, is one of the ancient thoroughfares outside the city walls, and was the centre of the old community of the parish of St Paul's Without the Walls. This church, basically of the 13th century, was probably built to serve the small community which grew up between the city walls and St Augustine's to serve the inhabitants of the abbey. The whole area suffered from German air raids in the 1939-45 war, though the basic structure of the church survived intact.

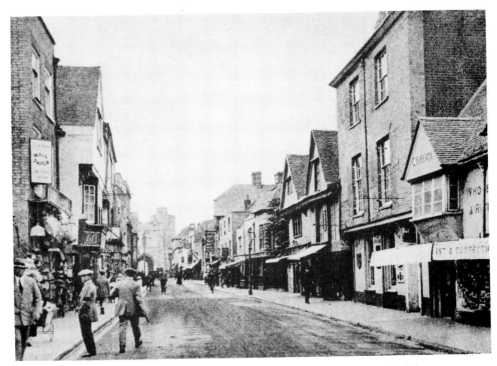

128. This reproduction of a postcard of 1917 shows St Peter's Street before the First World War, with the Westgate at the end of the street. The poor road surface, the lack of traffic and the many little shops should all be noted.

129. St Peter's Street, which stretches from the King's Bridge over the river as far west as the Westgate, is one of the city's oldest and most interesting streets. Travellers and pilgrims in early times came down from London on the Watling Street and so to the Westgate, through which they entered the city if they managed to arrive during daylight hours, since the gates were closed at sunset. In 1988 the street is constantly changing, older premises being replaced by brash new shop fronts at street level, though the ancient buildings are carefully preserved and are of great interest above the ground floor, with a variety of old fronts, gabled ends and tiled roofs.

130.   Mercery Lane in the middle years of the 19th century, probably in the 1860s. On the left are several surviving arches, and the jettying out of the upper storeys of surviving parts of the old Chequer of the Hope pilgrim hostel. In the bottom left-hand corner is the local office of the South Eastern Railway.

131. Mercery Lane is one of the best known and certainly one of the most ancient roads in the city, leading from the High Street to Christ Church Gate. Travellers and pilgrims of earlier centuries would have passed this way to the tomb of St Thomas in the great priory church. The whole of the left hand side of the lane was lined with an arcade of stone arches which supported the overhanging east walls of the Chequers of the Hope, the great pilgrim hospice. On the right-hand corner stood a fine old house, once owned by Soloman the Mercer, and the houses of mercers stretched down that side of the lane. Here the pilgrims bought souvenirs of their visit from the stalls under the arches, Canterbury fabrics for the women at home and perhaps for the village church, little lead bottles containing water mixed with the blood of the martyr, and lead brooches and pendants on which were representations of the head of the saint with the words *Caput Thomae*, before setting off on their long journey home.

132. & 133. It is hard to believe that these photographs of Ivy Lane were taken as recently as 1910. The old houses obviously lacking any adequate care or maintenance were of varied periods, but mostly of late 16th- or 17th-century origin. Note the absence of any street furniture or signs, one solitary gas lamp being the only concession to more modern times. In these houses, many of them little better than hovels, large families were brought up in great poverty. It is hardly surprising that chronic disease and illness was rampant.

Floods

134. Canterbury has always been very liable to flooding, being at or very near normal river level, and also because the city's watermills offered considerable resistance to the free flow of the river. Millers naturally kept their mill pools full of water so that they could operate successfully, and so any sudden storm water inevitably spilled out into the streets. However, the floods of 29 and 30 October 1909, though no doubt very distressing for those affected by them, supplied splendid flood photographs which show the pre-war state of some of the streets. This is Lower Bridge Street in 1909.

135.   Floods in North Lane, 1909.
136.   The 1909 floods in Blackgriffin Lane.

Shops & Markets

137.   The Boot's the Chemist shop in the High Street has a recorded history going back more than eight centuries to 1153, when Wilbert became prior of Christ Church and bought the land on the corner of Mercery Lane which he leased to Soloman the mercer, an important Canterbury businessman of that time. The building still contains work of several different periods, though much of what survives above ground is probably of the mid-15th century, but built over extensive stone cellars, probably two centuries earlier. It had to be much repaired in 1930, but this was done with enormous care to preserve the essential character of the building, which must be rated one of the finest surviving non-ecclesiastical structures of the city.

138. An 1887 photograph of the old Tudor house in the High Street known as Queen Elizabeth's Guest Chamber, which is claimed to date from 1573. Both the first and second floors are jettied out and the front of the second floor carries some fine pargetting. The house still survives, beautifully maintained, though a second bay has been added to the front of the first floor and a wrought-iron bracket now carries a nice representation of the head of Queen Elizabeth I.

139. This early 20th-century photograph shows the former *Star Inn*, which fronted the South Eastern Station Road. The *Rose and Crown Inn* is just discernible on the extreme right. The triple gable front was a feature of many old Canterbury buildings.

140. A 1915 photograph of a cooper's business in Burgate Street, exhibiting in its windows a wide variety of wooden containers.

141.   This 1880's photograph of the premises now known as 'the Weavers' is captioned 'Old Huguenot Houses on King's Bridge'. The sign reads 'Strand's Kings Bridge Steam dye works'.

142.   The fine old timber-framed Huguenot house now called 'the Weavers'. It carries a signboard claiming it dates from 1500, but other evidence suggests it was established later in the 16th century. The Canterbury weaving industry flourished after the arrival of the Huguenots and the Walloons, protestant refugees from religious persecution on the continent. They produced cottons, muslins, taffetas, velvets and, later, silks, none of which competed with the woollen broadcloths woven by the native Kentish weavers. Weaving in Canterbury reached its zenith in the middle of the 17th century, and the refugee weavers gave much work to Canterbury woolcombers, dyers and spinners, but by the early years of the 18th century the volume of trade had declined drastically. In recent years some craft weaving has again been done in this building.

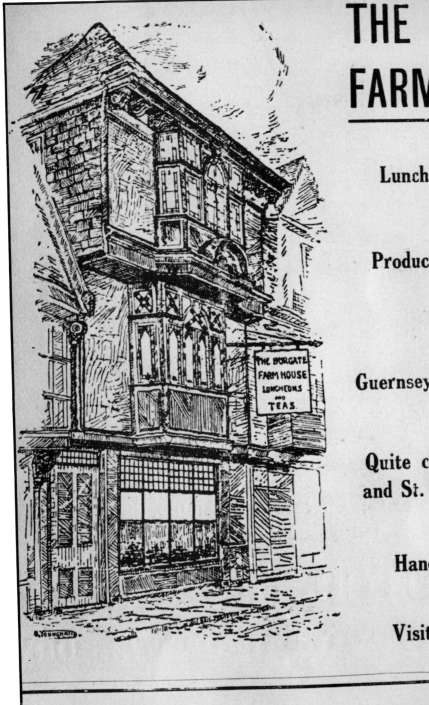

THE BURGATE FARMHOUSE.

Luncheons and Teas.

Produce from our own Farm.

Guernsey Milk and Butter.

Quite close to Cathedral and St. Augustine's Abbey.

Handy for Shoppers and Visitors to the City.

CONVENIENT CLOAKROOMS.

143. This advertisement of *c.*1930 illustrates how many of the needs of the city could then be supplied from local sources, in this case one of the farms in the vicinity which marketed its produce in its own shop in Burgate Street.

Houses

144.   This fine Tudor house in Palace Street, a listed building, is one of the most photographed in the city. The close-set members of its wooden frame, the double overhang of the front, and many detailed decorative features are all notable.

145. Sir Roger Manwood's house at St Stephen's, Hackington, drawn by Francis Grose F.S.A. in 1759. Sir Roger Manwood, who died in 1592, was a loyal servant of Queen Elizabeth I. He was Chief Baron of the Exchequer, and set up two charitable institutions, the Sir Roger Manwood Grammar School at Sandwich, and the Sir Roger Manwood Hospital at Hackington in 1590.

146. A fine old timber-framed house at St Stephen's, dated 1674 and photographed at the end of the 19th century.

147. Old houses in Burgate Street, mostly of the 16th or 17th century, now destroyed and replaced by modern shops, though the tower of St Mary Magdalene's church, seen in the distance, still survives.

148. An old drawing, dated 1901, of a window in the old *Fleur de Lis Inn*, long since demolished. The casement windows are jetted out from the wood-framed front wall surface and are supported by curious carved wooden ornamental brackets.

149. This excellent example of Tudor moulded brickwork was the old gateway, and all that remains of the great 16th-century Place House, the home of the Roper family. Its doorway has an elegant four centre arch of brick, over which is a prominent brick hoodmould, a triple light window and a stepped gable end. The decorative detail and the surface of all the brickwork, though in good condition when this photograph was taken in 1912, now suffers from considerable crumbling, the result of age and weather. In the 1530s it was the home of Master William Roper and his wife Margaret, who was the daughter of Sir Thomas More.

150.   This quaint old 17th-century building at the end of Palace Street, now used as the King's School shop, is a timber-framed structure, the framing infil being plaster made to look like stone. The unusual feature is that both the first and the second storeys overhang at the front and the right side, but not at the left, presumably because the left side was built tight up against an existing wall or building. The overhangs are supported on old, nicely carved, brackets. In early times it was known as the Old Dutch House but later it was said to have been the residence of Sir John Boys, though recent research has proved this to be very improbable.

151. A 19th-century photograph of a 17th-century house captioned 'Huguenot's House next Masonic temple, St Peter Street'. Note the Venetian window in the gable end of the left-hand house. The twin doors of the gable end of the right-hand house were usual in weavers' houses, the loft space under the roof being used for storage of wool and finished cloth. There were many such houses in the city and a number still survive.

152. The *House of Agnes Hotel* in St Dunstan's Street between the Westgate and the railway level crossing is a fine example of a timbered house, extremely well maintained, with a triple gable end overlooking the street, and a double overhang supported externally on the top overhang by attractive carved braces. It is traditionally associated with Charles Dickens, and is said to be the house of Mr. Wickfield in his book *David Copperfield*.

153. This little house (on the far left) in Chantry Lane was said to have been the model Charles Dickens used for Uriah Heep's house in *David Copperfield*.

Houses of Refreshment

154.   This large building, on the corner of Mercery Lane and the High Street, stands on the site of the ancient Chequers of the Hope, one of the principal hospices for the accommodation of travellers and pilgrims, not only to Canterbury itself, but also to Dover and on to the continent or even, perhaps, to the Holy Land. This inn was built specifically as a travellers' hospice by Prior Chillenden in the 15th century. It occupied practically the whole length of Mercery Lane and a similar distance down what is now the High Street, and consisted of buildings on all four sides of an open quadrangle, and a gallery, reached by a stairway, ran all round the interior to connect with the upper floors. Chaucer knew this hospice since he wrote that when his pilgrims arrived in Canterbury: 'They took their inn and lodged them at mid-morrow I trow/At the Chequers of the Hope that many a man doth know'. This was the dormitory of the hundred beds, the buttery, the pantry, the garden with its herbs and flowers of Chaucer's *The Supplementary Tale*, a place to be described, time and again, by pilgrims on their return to their homes.

155. This fine old drawing, probably of the 18th century, shows the interior courtyard of the old Chequers of the Hope pilgrim hospice and some surrounding accommodation.

156. This undated drawing shows a hall in the ancient Chequers of the Hope hospice, with its many windows, tie beams and crown post roof, all of late 14th- or early 15th-century date.

157. The old *Saracen's Head Inn* in Burgate Street in the 1930s. The tile-hung upper storey and gable ends was a very typical feature of Canterbury buildings. Many tile-hung buildings were of early timber-framed construction, and were later covered with tiles when they were no longer watertight.

158. The *George and Dragon Inn*. This old 17th-century building, with a double overhang at the front and first-floor bay windows, was a commercial house and sold Flint and Son's 'fine ales and porter'. It is shown here in 1899, shortly before it was demolished to provide a site for the Beaney Institute, which of course still survives on the same spot.

159.   The *Sun Hotel* in Sun Street, only a few yards from the Christ Church Gate, with its double overhang and some fine old woodwork, now much better kept than in this illustration of the beginning of the century, is one of the city's very distinctive buildings, dating from 1503. It may quite possibly have been a corner of the old Chequer of the Hope hostel. It was not, however, the original inn. This, according to G. M. Rainbird in his *Inns of Kent*, was a building next to the Christ Church Gate, the tenant in 1205 being a man named Wimund. Later, it seems, this inn was called the *Sun Tavern* and remained as such in 1661, but by 1667 the building was used for other purposes, so around that time the inn was probably removed to its present site. The *Sun* figured in Charles Dickens' *David Copperfield* as the 'Little Inn' where Mr. Micawber stayed, and where his three supporters met him on their way to expose Uriah Heep. Note that in its wall publicity it claimed to have 'Good accommodation for cyclists' and 'Good stabling'. The age of the motorcar had not then arrived.

160. The *Flying Horse Inn*, 1888. This old inn, in Dover Street, was once an important link in the great network of stage coaches. There were several *Flying Horse Inns* on the Dover, Canterbury and London route, but the Dover one has disappeared and this one at Canterbury may be the sole survivor. It is now in excellent condition.

161. The *Three Tuns Hotel*. At the junction of St Margaret's Street and Castle Street stands this fine and well-maintained building nearly four centuries old. Its overhanging upper storey is topped by a shallow pitched roof almost hidden behind the walls which are extended upwards to form a parapet. The word 'Tun' derives from the old Saxon 'tunne', a container. Later however 'tun' was more particularly used to describe a barrel holding 252 wine gallons. The sign hanging from the front of the hotel illustrates three such wine barrels.

162. The ancient *Falstaff Inn*, one of Kent's finest, still stands just outside the Westgate. It has been claimed that it dates from 1406 but many of its details suggest a later date. It is a fine old timber-framed house with much carved and oak-panelled work. In the 18th century it was an important coaching inn, and its through-passage for the horse-drawn coaches still survives. Standing outside the Westgate and the city walls, it was free from the domination of the ecclesiastical and civic authorities suffered by other hostelries within the walls. It was also a great convenience for travellers between London and Dover, especially those who reached the city after the gates were closed for the night. Many years after it first opened the inn was renamed the *Falstaff* after Shakespeare's famous character.

War Damage

163.   Though the quality is not good, this is one of the few views now available of a part of the city which was completely destroyed by enemy bombing in the 1939-45 war. It is one of St George's Street *c*.1909. All that now remains is the church tower in the centre of the picture.

164.   Old St George's church after the air raid which destroyed it. The masonry of the Perpendicular Gothic window survived and the clock was largely undamaged. Only the old west tower now survives, the body of the church having been cleared away and the site redeveloped.

165.   Looking over the Longmarket after the bombing in the Second World War. The south-west turret of the Bell Harry is enclosed in scaffolding and the barrage balloons still fly over the city.

166.   Evidence of one small part of the human cost of the war, the stone tablet at the Kent and Canterbury Hospital to the memory of Staff Nurse Bragg and Nurse Fairfax-Brown, two of many who gave their lives.

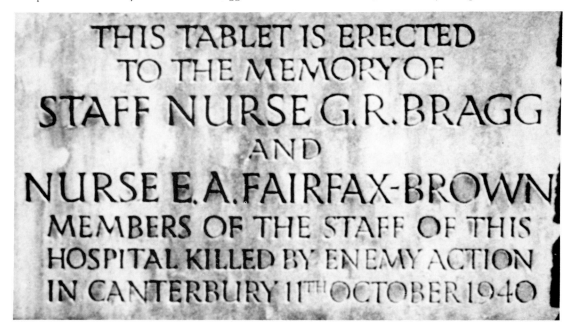

THIS TABLET IS ERECTED
TO THE MEMORY OF
STAFF NURSE G.R.BRAGG
AND
NURSE E.A.FAIRFAX-BROWN
MEMBERS OF THE STAFF OF THIS
HOSPITAL KILLED BY ENEMY ACTION
IN CANTERBURY 11TH OCTOBER 1940

Commerce

167.   The Mintyard Gate, dated 1545, is a reminder that Canterbury, like other major cities and towns, had its own mints in early times. The first English pennies, which were to be the standard unit of currency in England for centuries, were struck for the great King Offa in the eighth century by Canterbury mints, which continued to function for a further eight centuries. Gordon Kopley, in his annotation of Camden's *Britannia*, Kent, notes that the laws of Athelstan issued at Grateley (924-39) state: 'In Canterbury. (there are to be) seven moneyers; four of the king, two of the bishop, one of the abbot ...'. Later some of the city moneyers became rich and important men as, for instance, did Lambin Frese and Wiulf the Rich, among others.

168. The famous *Invicta*, a remarkable pioneer locomotive, was built by Robert Stephenson and Co. at Newcastle in 1830 for the Canterbury to Whitstable Railway. This marked a great step forward in locomotive design. Its multi-tubular boiler with copper tubes, coupled wheels and forward-placed cylinders driving back to cranks on the wheels set a precedent or all locomotives built afterwards. It had two cylinders, one on each side of the boiler, each with a bore of 10 inches and a stroke of 18 inches. The boiler, eight feet long and 40 inches in diameter, worked at a pressure of 40 to 50 pounds per square inch. For many years the locomotive was exhibited out in the open and suffered much deterioration, but in 1977 it was taken to the National Railway Museum for restoration and is now housed in the Poor Priests' Hospital museum. The photograph shows the *Invicta* before restoration.

169. The Canterbury West Railway Station was one of a number built in 1846 on the new North Kent Line of the South Eastern Railway from Ashford to Margate. This station may have been the work of architect Samuel Beazley. It is simple and well proportioned, a single-storey building with a shallow pitched hipped roof hidden by a surrounding parapet. The open recessed space in the front has two fluted pillars and both sides are balanced by sash windows. Nearby was the terminus of the old Canterbury to Whitstable Railway which later became part of the South Eastern Railway system until it was finally closed in 1954.

170. Claimed to be the first steam locomotive-hauled passenger railway in the world, the Canterbury to Whitstable line was opened on 3 May 1830 and continued in service until 1954. It ran from near the harbour at Whitstable to a point close to the present Canterbury West station, on the front of which this plaque is attached. Because of the severe gradients of the line at both ends, the little *Invicta* steam locomotive could haul the trains only on the relatively flat plateau through Blean. Both end sections had to be worked by ropes pulled by stationary engines.

NEAR HERE WAS THE TERMINUS
OF THE
CANTERBURY AND WHITSTABLE
RAILWAY, 1830
(GEORGE STEPHENSON, ENGINEER)
THE WORLD'S FIRST RAILWAY
SEASON TICKETS ISSUED HERE 1834

Frequent Expresses

and Cheap Fares to

CANTERBURY

from LONDON (Victoria, Charing Cross) daily

CHEAP FARES from LONDON

WEEK-END TICKETS (Friday-Tuesday)		HOLIDAY TICKETS (on various days during the Summer)
1st Class	3rd Class	Return Fare
17/6	**10/6**	**10/6** 3rd Class

See the District!

Cheap Day Tickets from CANTERBURY by numerous trains daily, as under:—

	s. d.		s. d.
ASHFORD	2/-	MAIDSTONE, EAST ...	4/6
BROADSTAIRS	2/6	(Weds., Sats., Suns.)	
DEAL	2/9	MARGATE	2/9
DOVER	2/6	MINSTER JCT.	1/9
FOLKESTONE...	2/3	RAMSGATE	2/3
HASTINGS	5/3	LONDON	8/-
HYTHE	2/6	(Weekdays except Sats.)	

Available for return on day of issue by any train.

Take a 7-DAY "HOLIDAY SEASON"

obtainable on demand any day during the Summer at any Station between Canterbury, Dover, Margate, etc., and available for seven days, including date of issue, at all Stations in the area covered.

TRAVEL WHEN— WHERE — and AS OFTEN as you like.

10/6 3rd Cl.

Children under 14 HALF-PRICE.

Programmes at S.R. Stations.

For full particulars of Trains, Service, Cheap Tickets, etc., apply at local S.R. Stations, or to Traffic Manager (Commercial), Southern Railway, London Bridge Station, S.E. 1.

SOUTHERN RAILWAY

171. A 1930s advertisement for the old Southern Railway, one of the four groups created from 120 independent railways by the passing of the Railways Act in 1921. The prices make interesting reading.

172. This fine old Columbian printing press stands outside the offices of the *Kentish Gazette* in St George's Place and I am indebted to the newspaper for the following details. The first iron press to be marketed in America, it was invented by George Clymer in 1813 in Philadelphia, but it was a commercial failure there and Clymer moved to England in 1817. From 1829 the firm, based in London, was known as Clymer and Dixon and made presses which were sold both in England and on the continent. Production continued certainly until the end of the 19th century.

173. Though not very clear, the name plate of the Columbian press indicates that it was No. 721 and that it was made in London in 1836. It seems therefore that it was one that was made by the parent firm of Clymer and Dixon, and not by another firm. When it was first used by the *Kentish Gazette* is not clear, but it continued to be used for many years, and even produced page proofs of the newspaper until the early 1960s.

174.   Standing at the front of the *Three Tuns Hotel* at the corner of
Watling Street and Castle Street is this reminder of the time when most
towns organised their own electricity supply system. It is a solid cast-
iron box with a fine representation of the city's arms on the locked front
door.